To Jonathan —

    I am grateful
for all that you have
brought into my life.
you are a generous and
inspiring friend.
    More journeys together!

          Love,

        Fritz

September 1993

EARTH
& SPIRIT

EARTH
& SPIRIT

The Spiritual Dimension
of the Environmental Crisis

Edited by FRITZ HULL

Foreword by THOMAS BERRY

CONTINUUM · NEW YORK

To Timothy Hull
May you and your generation take the lead.

1993
The Continuum Publishing Company
370 Lexington Avenue, New York, NY 10017

Printed in the United States of America

Library of Congress Cataloging-in-Publication Data

Earth & spirit : the spiritual dimension of the environmental crisis
  / edited by Fritz Hull ; foreword by Thomas Berry.
      p.   cm.
  Includes bibliographical references.
  ISBN 0-8264-0575-4 (hbd. : alk. paper)
    1. Human ecology—Religious aspects.   2. Environmental
degradation—Religious aspects.   I. Hull, Fritz.
  II. Title: Earth and spirit.
  GF80.E17   1993
  291.1'78362—dc20   93-424
                                                           CIP

This book is printed on acid-free recycled paper.

Contents

Preface

by FRITZ HULL

A s the sun appears over the crest of the Cascade Mountains, streams across the water, and pours into my living room, it is hard to feel the world so beset by abuse and destruction. Maybe in that moment of sunrise it is important not to have such feelings, so that beauty has the chance to inspire hope, and hope inspire creativity. But not long after the sun has risen, the full light of day and the newspaper remind me that the natural world I have grown so to love, is suffering incalculable degradation.

As I watch the environmental crisis worsening, it is becoming clear that the roots of the problem run deep. Fundamental questions are being raised about the purpose and impact of human life upon the Earth and about the actions our species must take in the crucial years ahead.

Until recently, the spiritual dimension of the ecological crisis has been largely ignored. Today, this is changing. Many people, including numerous religious, environmental, and political leaders, now believe that the ecological crisis is preeminently a spiritual crisis of the greatest magnitude. Its resolution depends on a basic transformation of human hearts and minds . . . a profound reshaping of how we think and live so that we may deepen our kinship with all life, create a new vision of human presence within the Earth community, and craft new patterns of ecological wholeness and human justice.

This book is based on the conviction that the spiritual dimension of life provides a relatively untapped reservoir of wisdom, imagination, and strength for meeting the challenge of a damaged Earth and for calling humanity into a new relationship with the natural order. The spiritual dimension offers the depth needed to understand this crisis, the courage to confront destructive patterns, the commitment and staying power to engage this crisis over the long haul, and a hopeful spirit from which a new and sustainable culture may be born. This makes understanding the spiritual dimension of the environmental crisis a matter of great urgency. The health and quality of life on the planet are now at stake.

Seeking to comprehend this time of ecological peril, we as the human presence on the planet need a depth of insight and a wisdom that exceeds our own, that will take us to the true heart of our dilemma, and that will guide us in seeking solutions. Increasingly there are public figures who make reference to spirituality. Words like *sacred* and *spiritual* are now heard in common discourse about the Earth. The secretary general of the United Nations, Boutros Boutros-Ghali, speaking at the Earth Summit in Rio de Janeiro in June 1992, remarked: "To the Ancients, nature was the dwelling place of the gods. The Earth had a soul. To find that soul and restore it, this is the essence of Rio." The increase in such explicit references to religion or spirituality indicates a quest for depth of insight into what has gone wrong, and a greater wisdom as how now to act. We clearly are on the search for a way of seeing and knowing that will surpass conventional understanding and that will contain no falsehood, no distortion, and no nonsense. We are looking for something qualitatively different from what we have known, that will provide a radical reshaping of the way we learn to value and make choices.

Today the word *spiritual* is being freed from associations that have been restrictive and laden with religious dogma. For many, the word carries an association that is less personalistic and self-focused than in times past. It often refers now to a more collective experiencing of the numinous or sacred quality of Earth. It preserves an openness to the mystery of the universe, to God, and to the essential importance of a vision of life infused with a sense of the sacred. Increasingly this word suggests that which touches our deepest instincts, pierces our illusions, and opens us to everything in the world that expresses love and truth.

The new use of the word *spiritual* corresponds with the profound questing for spiritual experience under way in this culture. At the time when conventional religious ideas and institutions are diminishing in power and influence, the immediate experience of nature is becoming a source of spiritual vitality. This raises a host of theological issues and challenges to institutionalized religion.

My own spiritual journey led me into a theological education and ordination into the ministry, and for this I remain grateful. In my earlier world of theology and church life, "nature" was seldom referenced, and was never considered a source of spiritual perspective or empowerment. But my personal experience in nature aroused and nourished my inmost spirit and forced theological reconsiderations. Often I kayak the waters of Puget Sound and journey even further north along the wilderness coast of British Columbia and Alaska. These, as well as other experiences in the forests, mountains, and islands of the Pacific Northwest, have awakened in me a profound desire for a new way of relating to the natural order . . . or creation. For many years I carried with me these words by Chief Dan George that expressed my feeling better than anything I could find:

> The beauty of the trees,
> the softness of the air,
> the fragrance of the grass,
>   speaks to me.

> The summit of the mountain,
> the thunder of the sky,
> the rhythm of the sea,
>   speaks to me.

> The faintness of the stars,
> the freshness of the morning,
> the dewdrop on the flower,
>   speaks to me.

The strength of fire,
the taste of salmon,
the trail of the sun,
and the life that never goes away,
    they speak to me.

And my heart soars.[1]

The idea and inspiration for this book springs in part from my
own experience in the wilderness, and the intensity of my personal
need to explore the spiritual dimension of nature and the environmental crisis.

This book also issues from an exceptionally powerful conference
in Seattle in 1990 entitled "Earth and Spirit." The conference was
sponsored by the Chinook Learning Center, a twenty-year-old,
innovative, educational center and community on Whidbey Island.
At that time I was a codirector of Chinook and a principle organizer
of the conference. Many of the contributors to this book served as
conference faculty, and some of the material for the book was first
offered in major addresses or in workshops.

One reason for the success of the conference was that we were
willing to tackle head-on the deeply implicit, but not very explicit,
connection between the environmental crisis and the deeply felt
need for spiritual perspective and response. Many people were
ready for fresh thinking and experience that would begin to forge
this connection. The many Native American participants in the
conference were able to demonstrate the intrinsic link between
Earth and Spirit, even questioning the use of the word *and* in the
title. To them the two realities are interwoven parts of each other.
This book is an extension of the spirit, gift, and challenge of the
conference.

Earth & Spirit seeks to interpret the challenge of the ecological
crisis, to suggest a new understanding of the relationship between
God, humanity, and nature, and to urge the development of values
and action strategies that will create a sustainable future for planet
Earth. It upholds the values of eco-justice . . . the ongoing linkage
of ecology and justice. A variety of theological and spiritual perspectives are reflected in this book. However, it has not been my

intention, as editor, to represent all major faith traditions or all prominent perspectives that today are addressing this subject. As the book developed it became evident that such would not be achieved in a single volume. The contributors to this book are people whom I have met along the way, many of them colleagues and close friends. In this respect the book has become a sort of family project. Included among the contributors are a theologian, psychotherapist, vocalist, poet, mailman, cathedral dean, fisherman, artist, estuary consultant, journalist, priest, and biologist. Some are seasoned writers and some are risking spirit in written form for the first time. The book is filled with the inspiration of many voices and professions, all speaking to the need to create a new relationship *with* the natural world and to take care of it.

It is my deep hope that these well-considered words of many friends will further the great conversation now under way, that they will have all of us talking of these things, not only with ourselves and each other, but with the trees as well. I believe that we are being called and led by God's Spirit, and by the Earth itself, to live with a new sense of wonderment, respect, and love for the world. With heightened spiritual sensitivities we must create the ways in which we will live on this planet, ensuring a healthy and equitable future for human life and for all parts of creation.

Foreword

by THOMAS BERRY

In this late twentieth century we have suddenly awakened with a certain ecstatic delight to the intimate presence of a vast community of beings that are all speaking to us, delighting in our single community of existence, celebrating with us each dawn and sunset. This capacity of every being to shape its own identity, to declare its delight in being, its joy in the universe with song and dance, with movement over the Earth, or in the air, or through the sea; this capacity to establish intelligible patterns of action, to influence and be influenced by others, the capacity to evoke in humans their participation in the ultimate mysteries of the universe through song and dance and ritual—this is a spirit dimension functioning in and through the visible, tangible world about us.

Because we have not understood this, for centuries we experienced the universe as a collection of objects to be exploited rather than as subjects with which we commune. The universe about us, desacralized, without inherent dignity, with no rights, no voice, no freedom to be itself, its spirit presence denied, became the victim of relentless assault in its every aspect.

Although it took centuries to learn the skills for exploiting the resources of the planet for human convenience, this was eventually achieved. The devastation that we have brought upon the forests, the rivers, the seas, the air, and all the biosystems of the planet is stunning in its enormity. Only recently have we recognized that the stress we are placing on the planet is more than the planet can endure—that we are ourselves enveloped in the disintegration that we are causing.

Suddenly we recognize that we must rethink all our basic values, the structure and functioning of our entire cultural tradition, for these difficulties did not arise yesterday, nor out of Hindu or Buddhist or Confucian tradition. This moment of reappraisal is undoubtedly the most awesome moment for rethinking our situation since the beginning of the Western civilizational enterprise some five thousand years ago.

When European peoples came here in the sixteenth century there lived on the North American continent a vast number of tribal groups, some ten million persons in all, with a profound appreciation of the spirit dimension of the continent and their own place and role within the life community of the continent, a people who heard the voices of the mountains and valleys, the flowers in the meadows, the trees of the forest, the birds and other animals. The entire continent, with the celestial world above, was all a sacred place, the realm of the Great Mystery, designated as Orenda by the Iroquois, as the Manitou by the Algonquin, as Wakan Tanka by the Sioux.

There were rituals such as the Great Thanksgiving Ceremony of the Seneca, or the Sun Dance of the Western Tribes, or the rituals performed on special occasions, such as the Omaha ceremony performed at the birth of a child. Soon after birth the infant was presented to the universe while asking for the continued presence of the universe to this child throughout the course of its life. A multitude of other rituals were celebrated throughout the year. There were the dances, the Deer Dance and the Buffalo Dance and the Eagle Dance of the Plains Indians. In all of these the indigenous peoples entered into the spirit world where every mode of earthly being was recognized within the single sacred community of the universe itself.

How different from the attitude of the invading peoples from across the Atlantic who began to occupy this continent in the seventeenth century. These had sundered the earthly from the heavenly, the sacred from the profane, the human from the natural, the divine from the created, the Christian from the heathen, the saved from the unredeemed.

Yet there was a certain ambivalence in the European attitude, especially toward the natural world. This can be seen from the preaching of Jonathan Edwards indicating that the divine glory was revealed throughout the order of nature. Yet at the same time the dominant reference to the continent was as a dark and dangerous and somewhat demonic place that had to be conquered and controlled. It is little wonder that the exploitation of the continent for supposed human benefit throughout the past four centuries has met minimal resistance within Euro-American society. Even so, as early as the 1820s, James Fenimore Cooper was writing his Leatherstocking tales all dealing with the superficialities of civilization and the vigor of the wilderness. In the first of these, *Pioneers*, with its setting in the place of his birth in the upper reaches of the Susquehanna River in New York State, in the year 1793, he presents extensive defense of the forest based not on conservation principles of humans, or on some stewardship attitude, but on the sacred right of the forest to exist and fulfill its proper role in the larger pattern of the Earth community. Fenimore Cooper recognized the nobility of the indigenous peoples and the validity of their sense of this sacred aspect of the universe in the variety of its manifestations. This attitude could not be further developed in Cooper's time because of an extreme alienation from the natural world manifested by the incoming Europeans and their attachment to the biblical revelation as the unique divine manifestation. What is clearly stated in the writings of Cooper is the devastating impact the Europeans were having on the natural life systems of the continent, on the forests, and all forms of wildlife.

The despoiling of the soil is also the principal complaint of William Strickland who journeyed up the Hudson River in the year 1793. Speaking of the settlers in the region he writes, "The barbarous backwoodsman has got possession of the soil, and fire and the axe are rapidly levelling the woods. The backwoodsman has an utter abhorrence for the works of the creation, that exist on the place where he unfortunately settles himself." These tendencies have marked the American attitude toward the native peoples of this continent and the attachment to a mechanistic sense of the natural world, not to a sense of the inherent sacred quality of natural phenomena.

A more profound feeling for the continent emerges in the late eighteenth and the beginning of the nineteenth century, the period generally identified as the romantic period in Western cultural history. While this movement was dominated by its philosophical and religious emphasis, it did achieve an intimate rapport with the spirit presence manifested throughout the natural world.

In the religious, philosophical context the Transcendentalist Movement established in the American mind an awareness of being a new people in a new land. When Ralph Waldo Emerson presented his first complete study for American academic life in the form of his essay on Nature this inaugurated a new period in human Earth relations on this continent. He saw the natural world as expressive of transcendent spirit. This awakening to the natural world was considered at the time as heretical, pagan, gnostic, pantheistic, naturalistic. Out of this movement came Henry Thoreau and later John Muir, both of whom had deep feelings for the spirit quality of the natural world in its specific American expression.

While these gave expression to the American scene in writing out of a European-derived transcendentalism, a more fundamental appreciation of the American continent and the native peoples of the continent was taking place through the work of such artists as Karl Bodmer and George Catlin. Karl Bodmer traveled with Prince Maximilian of Weid up the Missouri River in the years 1833–34 and recorded in his paintings the outstanding Indian persons and scenes that he met, a collection that is considered without equal in documenting such early people prior to their coming under modern European influences. The reverence manifested in these paintings gives evidence of a profound regard the painter had for both the peoples and the scenes he was recording.

In somewhat the same time, 1830–36, George Catlin went through the region of the Plains Indians painting the portraits of the people and the scenes of daily life. In his narrative also he reveals what might be considered the sunset glory of the Indians of this region. This is in strange contrast with the negative view of the Indian as found in the actual negotiations with the Indians, with the inability of the Europeans to give any proper justice to these tribal peoples in regard to their persons, their land, or their way of life.

Also in the painting of the Hudson River School in the mid-nineteenth century we discover a new sense of the wonder of the continent expressed in the luminous paintings of Thomas Cole,

Frederick Church, and Asher Durand. The various scenes of the river were expressed in a magnificent tide of light sweeping over the entire scene. Light of such brilliance had never before been seen in the paintings of this country. Here a certain humanistic aesthetic is joined to the sense of an abiding spiritual presence.

In the academic realm there existed also a deep interest in the native peoples and their sense of the spiritual dimension of this continent. But already a secular mood had taken over the American mind, the rise of an industrial society was in process. The mission of the Euro-American people was seen in the sociopolitical rather than in the spiritual order. An autism had settled over the American mind in relation to the natural world. This alienation was a prerequisite for the industrial assault on the continent that was underway.

Later, in the last half of this century, our human relation with the Earth would be dominated by the Conservation movement under the leadership of such men as Gifford Pinchot and President Theodore Roosevelt. While this did not adequately deal with the more profound rapport of humans with the natural world, it did recognize that the destinies of the human and those of the forest were intimately related. For the time it was the only protection that existed for the wildlife of the continent and its spiritual presence. Soon the continent would become so debased by industrial exploitation it could communicate a sense of the sacred only in a diminished manner.

Most profoundly at this time was the work of Herman Melville, *Moby-Dick*. This account of the pathological pursuit of the great white whale seen as a demonic power by Captain Ahab, illustrates the basic feeling of the American people that there was a frightening aspect of the natural world, a demonic presence that was to be feared and, where possible, destroyed. The natural world became sacralized only by human use. Wilderness, the demonic, paganism, seduction—these all went together.

The sense of the spirit presence within the natural world was not helped by the rise of academic studies of the natural world that occurred in the nineteenth century. The alienation was only increased. The further story concerns the work of George Perkins Marsh (1801–82) about Man and Nature. This was a landmark work that dealt only with the more academic questions. By this time it was clear that the entire organic world formed a single integral life system, that nothing in the biosystems of the planet existed apart from the other biosystems, that these were interrelated not only in their origin but also in their functioning. This was the period of academic reflection on the question of ecosystems, a term first used by the English scholar, Arthur George Tansley in 1935, although the concept had been developed much earlier.

The Earth and Spirit Conference in Seattle was symbolic of a new stage in our American relations with the continent, with the native peoples of this continent, and with the entire Earth community. These three constitute for us the three basic components of our sacred community. This rising tide of consciousness had its beginning long ago deep in the paleolithic period when humans first awakened to the experience of the natural world. In the unconscious depths of the human psyche we are all primal peoples. No people are without their profound memories of this earliest period of their existence. What is unique is that we are awakening anew out of a period of forgetfulness. The ever-present origin moment is making itself felt within us with a new vividness.

There is a deep pain within us as we awaken to the torment that we have been enduring all this time, for with the desecration of the outer world has come a corresponding loss to the inner world of the human. We lost our poetry. We estranged ourselves from all that could activate the more sublime inspirations within us. Our poets struggled to recover this presence to the natural world: Ralph Waldo Emerson, Emily Dickinson, Walt Whitman, Sidney Lanier, Edgar Allan Poe, and then finally Robinson Jeffers, the most powerful of our nature poets.

Finally we begin to recover our dreamworld, our imagination, the music of the universe, the color of the autumn leaves, the scarlet and blue and gold of the feathered creatures, and the humming sound of the insects. Although it is only a faint expression of what it once was, we still can recognize and participate in the song and dance that is going on around us.

We begin to envy those indigenous peoples of this continent who still keep their sensitivity, who still hear the voices of the universe, who still dance to the rhythms of the Earth. Their drumbeat still resounds throughout the planet, albeit in a manner more hushed from what it had been in earlier times. The dignity of the indigenous peoples still shines forth. Despite all that has happened they still maintain their inner formation of soul, of mind—a mind formation that expresses, apparently, an indestructible psychic determination. Their refusal to accept the patterns of meaning brought over from Europe was at first baffling to the occupiers of the country. But gradually, through the studies of tribal peoples, the perception they have of the spirit presence throughout the natural world begins to be understood.

Above all this was the period of domestication. To bring things under control of humans, this became the Euro-American ideal. We little realized that domestication was a despiritualization, the irretrievable loss of the most profound experiences available to humans. In their natural setting even the animals have a personality, a grandeur, an independence, a grace, a spontaneity, a beauty that domesticated animals never attain. But somewhere deep within the human soul there remains the longing for wilderness. That is what is now coming to expression. The human mode of life has been overwhelmed by mechanization, by money values.

In a sense we are returning to a situation that existed originally throughout the planet. The intimacy with the universe that existed in the late paleolithic period still exists in the depths of our minds. This period with its mysterious cave paintings was, in a sense, the crossover moment, the time when human development would occur in an immediacy with the surrounding spirit world of nature, an experience that can never be completely lost for it is the primordial basis of our existence as humans.

This book, like the Seattle conference, is an evocation, not an imposition. It represents a cosmological and historical urgency called forth from the entire Earth community. Neither the planet Earth nor the human community can any longer endure the impasse brought about by the isolation of the Earth in its physical reality from the spirit presences that give both to the Earth and its human community their true grandeur.

✦ *1* ✦

The Power of the Well-Packed Question

by VIVIENNE HULL

Accccording to the Irish tradition from which I come, it is said that "you get wise by asking questions, for the well-packed question carries its answer on its back, as a snail carries its shell. . . . For when you must yourself answer the problem that you have posed, you will meditate your question with care and frame it with precision . . . and come to understand by what successions a good question grows at last to a good answer."[1]

Let's hope the Irish are right. Like many others I am certain that we are living in the era of the well-packed question. While, in this last decade of the twentieth century, we maneuver our way through our own personal quest for meaningful and purposeful life for ourselves and our families, we are also confronted by questions of a far greater order of magnitude than people before us have had to answer—questions that, if we are to have hope for the future, we must believe carry their answers on their back.

People of other generations have certainly struggled with ultimate issues, and it is by the light of their discoveries and breakthroughs that we are now helped to find our way. There have been other periods like our own, characterized by unprecedented growth, uncertainty, and change, and the consequent inability of prevailing social, political, and religious institutions to hold together under the pressure of new discoveries and challenges. But the situation

19

we face as Western people of the 1990s is unmatched in a number of ways.

First, is the enormity of the present destruction of the natural environment, the consequent degradation of life for vast numbers of people and species, and the uncertain shadow this casts over the future of civilization, and of the planet itself. We are only now beginning to take this in. Maurice Strong, secretary-general of the United Nations Conference on Environment and Development that I attended in Rio de Janeiro in 1992, shared his conviction that in times past "civilizations have risen and fallen, and their effects have been momentous in local terms, but never in global terms. The difference today is that the whole global system of civilizations is in danger, and if we go through the process of decline and demise, that would be the end of our species on this planet."[2]

A second unprecedented factor influencing our time is that the environmental crisis is of our own making—and that we know it. The destruction of the environment is the price tag on the "standard of living" to which we have become accustomed, the "good life" that the rest of the world now holds up as their deserved future. We did not intend this. Though signs and warnings have been ample in the last two decades, the majority of us did not foresee that the way we conducted normal, daily life would result in the destruction of the natural environment to the point where the viability of fruitful life for our children and for theirs would be at threat. We know that the crisis of the environment is not an "act of God" or a "natural disaster." It is a consequence of our own values, beliefs, and choices.

And third, if all future life hinges on the choices men and women make now, in the decade of the 1990s, we know that there is no simple resolution to our questions if we are to turn our society in a new and life-sustaining direction. The answers we need will be found only in the deepest reservoirs of the human spirit as we look for a new wisdom about who we are, why we are here, and what is our appropriate place on this planet we call home.

Certain periods in history, like our own, are unique in that they are characterized by a pivotal transformation in the way people think about themselves and their world. Something breaks into human experience. Prevailing thought forms, belief systems, and concepts about life are brought to question. Such times are in no way easy for they are marked by a high degree of insecurity and anxiety as old ways break down and people struggle to figure out what is happening and how best to respond. Transition eras, however, also carry a tremendously creative power, as the imagination of new possibilities encourages an innovative and pioneering spirit.

At these bridge, or hinge times, men and women face enormously complex decisions. In the rush of events and the pressure of conflicting opinions about what is happening, we must choose which way to orient our lives. We have to decide whether we will work to maintain and shore up the familiar, though eroding, order of things, or commit our creative energy to the potential for a different future, even though its patterns and forms are undefined and unproven. How we answer the basic questions about which way the world is going and how we therefore choose to live, makes all the difference in how the future unfolds.

Noting the rare opportunities of such times, Hannah Arendt urged that we "pay close attention to the 'odd in-between period' which sometimes inserts itself into historical time, when not only the later historians but the actors and witnesses, the living themselves, become aware of an interval in time which is altogether determined by things that are no longer, and by things that are not yet. . . . In history, these intervals have shown more than once that they may contain the moment of truth."[3]

Now the Irish would also say that following that moment of truth, going after the resolution to the questions of the age, can become "the wobbliest of all occupations." It can become the philosopher's—or the cynic's—game, an excuse for the unwillingness to make the questions our own, and to stay with them to the point of decision, commitment, and action. However, when we understand that we are not dealing with abstract or remote issues, that our lives actually depend on what we decide and what we choose to believe, we grapple with our questions in a very different way.

When I think about the journey of my own life, and that of many of my closest colleagues and friends over the last two decades, I would say that all of us made pivotal decisions based on how we intuited or "hunched" what was our best response to troubling questions. We were unsettled by what was happening in our world, particularly by issues of war, racial and religious prejudice, and the environment. Many of us were also disturbed by what we perceived in many people as the erosion of a basic sense of purpose and confidence in life, a loss of direction, and a terrible hunger for something more than a materialistic and success-oriented society proffered. Much that had been in place for our parent's generation was not in place anymore for us. We knew that the questions we were asking would not be answered by waiting to arrive at "factual truth," nor by simplistic responses, for they were ultimately questions of values, meaning, and faith. Their resolution would not come from any outside authority, but only from the activation of our own inner intuitive sense of what was right and what must prevail. They were, in fact, the well-packed questions of the heart, and of the soul.

The energy of what disturbed us gave power to our quest, and to the choices we made. Most of us went for the future. We became involved in a creative assortment of endeavors in almost all fields, including education, agriculture, medicine, community development, business, and religion. Our questions led the way and the answers we needed revealed themselves as we went to work on behalf of what we most loved, and what we believed to be the highest truth we could follow.

So it is again today. The crucial questions raised by the unprecedented threat to our planet's ecology are both disturbing and energizing. We are again brought back to soul-level issues that are utterly personal and immediate. How did we come to the point where we are destroying the world? Why do so many still refuse to recognize or acknowledge this? Why is it so hard to change course? How do we learn to reconnect with the natural world and take our place with other species in a manner that is mutually life enhancing and sustaining? And perhaps the most fundamental question of all: how can we learn to extend our understanding and perception of the Sacred beyond the story of human experience and into the story of the Earth and the larger community of planetary life?

Following the trail of these well-packed questions brings us, I believe, up against the basic story we tell about who we are, where we are, and why we are. For the potential ruin of the planet's ecology did not happen merely because we made an ignorant or regretful choice along the way. We are in the state we're in because of fundamental assumptions we have been taught and the values and behaviors they support. It is here where the most crucial changes must happen, and must happen soon, if we are to avoid a twenty-first century characterized by unimaginable, and unconscionable, ecological degradation. The power of our beliefs to affect the world has never been more clearly apparent.

In an address to an interfaith symposium on "Spirit and Nature" held at Middlebury College in 1990, Christian theologian Sally McFague shared her conviction that changing what we believe about ourselves, others, and our planet is absolutely essential to healing the environment, and is one of the most important theological tasks we face today. Learning to think differently precedes being willing and able to act differently. She states:

> Western culture was and still is profoundly formed by the Hebrew and Christian religions and their stories, images, and concepts regarding the place of human beings, history, and nature in the scheme of things. [Its major images and metaphors] hold a power that is deep and old, therefore, difficult to discard, [yet], is dangerous in our time, for it encourages a sense of distance from the world, is concerned only with human beings, and supports attitudes of either domination of the world or passivity toward it. . . . No matter how ancient a metaphorical tradition may be, and regardless of its credentials in scripture, liturgy, and creedal statements, it still *must be discarded if it threatens the continuation and fulfillment of life.*" [Italics mine][4]

Arriving at a new guiding narrative, a story that enables us to "understand the place of human beings on our planet as one of radical interrelationship and interdependence with all other forms of life, and that reasserts the intimate and immanent participation of God in creation,"[5] may be among the most important occurrences of our time. Again, this is not an abstract exercise, but a profoundly personal and essential quest for us all.

I am quite sure that my own tale, and the well-packed questions of my life, though distinct in the particularity of place and event, are nonetheless familiar to many of my generation. I am the child of a tradition built on the separation of humankind from nature and God from the world, a tradition now being profoundly questioned in light of the planet's imperiled ecology.

My family was Irish, Protestant, and working class. From grandparents to parents, they made their way through the dislocations of this century, leaving the country for industrial Belfast in the hope of a better way of life for themselves and their children. They worked hard to raise their own standard of living and to be respectable and generous members of their community. They carried no conscious thought of harm to others, and lived by the assumption that success was measured by gains in material wealth, security, and the ability to provide opportunities for their children to do better than they themselves had done. They lived too, by the unchallenged belief that as we did better, so, somehow would everybody else. There was no ill intent here, only the unquestioned assumptions of a materially oriented, postwar society that equated the good life with good jobs, higher wages, and the production and consumption of goods.

We lived as well with the environment as a "taken for granted." We had no sense that the resources of nature would not always be there, providing more as we needed, nor that by living in the way we did, we were in any sense a detriment to the natural world. That was simply not part of the conversation at home, in school, in church, or in the political arena of the day. The natural world was valued as a source of necessary food and resources and an outlet for recreation. While nature's aesthetic qualities were regarded as of help to "man's soul," the land, or the salmon, the birds, or the forest creatures, the high fell, or the grove of oak or pine, had no intrinsic value in and of themselves. They were there to remind us of "God and His gifts."

The Church, fiercely Protestant, maintained these assumptions. While it offered the message of God's love and forgiveness, it was, in retrospect, strangely ignorant of the Irish countryside just outside its doors. It left its people cut off from the world around them, as if nature did not matter at all and played no part in the search of men and women for belonging, affection, meaning, and the enjoyment of one's life. It was, regrettably, overly suspicious of sensory experience, of the emotions, and of pleasure. It did not encourage an encounter with mystery or with awe. It did not foresee that what it taught as universal truth, would, in the span of my generation, not only prove inadequate for the spiritual and moral development of its people, but be called to account for the unconscionable abuse of the natural world.

The most damaging legacy of my early religious education was its insistence on a narrowly conceived redemption theology focused on concern for the salvation of the individual soul "out of this world." The Earth was not my home, so I was taught. I was a child of God, and God, according to Irish Presbyterianism, was not interested in anything but my soul. I belonged to the community of the saved, and if I made my way through the temptations of a fallen world, I would in time be "home," in Heaven, from which I had come. In some sense, therefore, I could have concluded that human beings were not natural to the planet. We came from somewhere else. We were here for just a short while, and with Christ's help, we would make it back to where we truly belonged. Later theological study would of course show me the error of oversimplified constructs about anything, and especially about Heaven, Hell, and the Earth. I would also come to a different understanding of the Christian story and the wisdom it can offer about the relationship between God and creation, between the spiritual and the material worlds. Nonetheless, the overly simplified version imprinted itself on my childhood mind. I have no doubt that the caricature carried in my head was also in the heads of many others—and continues still. It lives on in much of the conservative religious world, and in many of the basic premises of Western industrialized society.

It would hardly be fair to say that the religion of my younger life was without its wisdom and its gifts. While inadequate in crucial ways, it did provide an ethical framework centered on a basic knowledge of a loving and forgiving God who "knew me by name" and to whom I was ultimately accountable for my actions and my accomplishments. I grew up with an ethic of love and service as a paramount requirement for a moral life. It gave me too a sense of community to which I belonged, and it challenged me always to regard the needs and longings of others as equally, if not more, important than my own. Unfortunately, invitation and welcome did not extend to the Catholic neighbors, or the "non-Christians," or the "unchurched." That this prejudice represented a fundamental betrayal of Christianity's central moral ethic, and contributed tragically to the violence of Irish society, was either purposefully ignored or simply not understood.

Correspondingly, the prevailing view of earthly things as antagonistic to, or of less value than, the "things of God," resulted in a blatant disregard for the natural world and condoned the abuse of nature. The Church failed to recognize its complicity in the mounting degradation of the environment.

Even as a child, I knew that what I was being taught couldn't be wholly true. And as an adult, working hard to reframe and reform my theological premises with the Earth as primary context, it is to my childhood I return with the positive memory of experiences and sensibilities that, in truth, influenced me far more than the tight theology of Protestantism.

Like most children I loved the natural world. It was for me an environment of Grace. I wanted always to be outside, not in. I lived at the top of a "dead-end street," thus named because it "led nowhere." For me, however, it led everywhere. Once through the hedge at its end, I was out and off through the fields and the glens and into the foothills of the mountains near Belfast. Here I was at home, free, and happy. Here was the "real world," and it was here that, in the intuitive wisdom of the child, I understood that I was important, and needed in the larger scheme of things. Though I lacked a developed or cohesive spirituality, I knew, very simply, that the world around me was lit throughout with a bright and holy spirit. In an utterly unsophisticated manner, I believed unshakably that I must take care of it all because God had made it, and loved it too.

The Church's caution about pantheism came later as something of a shock. As a youngster I knew nothing of what it meant, and had no sense that I was "in danger of worshiping nature instead of God." Much later, of course, I came to understand that this was, and is, no small stumbling block for the Church on its road to the recovery of an environmental theology and ethic. The old fear of substituting nature for God remains a prickly issue for much of conservative Christianity. It is a primary reason for the exclusion of nature from mainstream theology and the reluctance of the

Church to respond to the environmental crisis as a religious issue. This is of course changing, albeit slowly.

While the intuitive wisdom of childhood does not always grow to a mature and guiding knowledge, the sense of sacred presence in nature has remained for me a foundational and guiding belief. Now, in the last years of the century, as more and more people awaken to the unprecedented crisis of the planet's environment, I am certain that a new recognition of the sacramentality of the natural world is essential.

As I searched for a theological framework adequate to my own experience of nature and of God, the rich diversity of the Christian tradition revealed its gifts. While the dominant Protestant theological perspective maintains the separation of divinity from the material world, with God and nature either overtly or subtly at odds, this is not the only way to tell the story. Within the larger Christian story there are streams of experience and theology in which God, humanity, and nature are intimate and mutually responsive partners in a sacred universe. They have been buried for a long while, but now are coming round again as we search for the roots of an ecologically responsible Christianity.

I struck gold in my own Irish tradition. It was an unexpected and marvelous discovery.

I knew nothing at all about Celtic Christianity until one summer, having given up on the Church and Calvinism, I spent time on the Island of Iona in Scotland and fell upon the story of the Irish monastic schools and the marvelous company of women and men through whose lives Christianity flourished and spread in the fourth, fifth, and sixth centuries. I had found my spiritual home at last.

Celtic Christianity, I learned, took root in second-century Ireland, in a culture with an ancient nature-oriented tradition that remained alive and vital. It was a culture that perceived the spiritual world as interpenetrating and interacting with the physical universe and accessible through the practical and immediate things of everyday life. Rather than break the connection to this older tradition, Celtic Christianity flourished by grafting to it the wisdom of its own new story. It developed a sophisticated theology that emphasized the immanent presence of God in all things and the sacramentality of the natural world. Each part of the created order was seen as an expression of the Divine and carried its own integral purpose and pattern. Humankind was responsible not only to God, but also to nature; the health or disease of the trees, animals, waters, and crops, were seen as a direct reflection of the harmony or disharmony of the human. Nature, the Celts believed, worked *with* humankind to restore and maintain the health and balance of the world.

For the Celts, the physical world was not the inanimate stage on which the human drama played itself out. Nor was nature merely a display of God's glory. The powers of nature—of wind and ocean, moon and sun, fire and lightning, trees and stones, plant and animal, and Earth itself—were understood to be directly responsive to human invocation. Throughout Celtic Christianity runs a constant sense of intimacy with the natural world and courtesy toward all its creatures. Everything in nature was seen as "living and powerful friends and companions (with) humankind as friend and companion to the world in which we live."[6] In Celtic Christianity nature was an active partner in the giving and receiving of praise and blessing.

So too were the angelic presences of the unseen spiritual realms. The sense of partnership and intimacy with the angelic world is as important to Celtic Christianity as its regard for the inherent integrity of the natural world. For these women and men there was no unbridgeable dichotomy between the visible and the invisible worlds, no perceived separation between matter and spirit. Instead, the invisible world was always near at hand and apprehensible to ordinary men and women. The older, mystical, animistic, and faery realm gained new meaning in the Celtic Christian world that took for granted that the angels of the Heavenly Kingdom were active and welcome presences in human affairs.

The Celtic attentiveness to the angelic realms and to nature did not mean a diminishment of the place and function of the Creator God. For the Celts, the Creator of the cosmos was not a "massive overshadowing presence, but a vibrant, all-sustaining, all-permeating energy. . . . The Triune God with the Heavenly Host and the marvelous creation of Earth and sky and ocean [was] a living intimate presence, the 'divine milieu' of Teilhard de Chardin, the 'breathing together of all things' of which the first philosophers of the West spoke so feelingly."[7]

This mystical intimacy of human, nature, and the divine that characterizes the essence of the Celtic Christian tradition is wonderfully illustrated in an eighth-century prayer credited to St. Patrick. Since Patrick was at work in the first half of the fifth century trying, unsuccessfully, to organize the dispersed Celtic church into the ecclesiastical pattern of the Roman world, this prayer could not have been his. Yet, it is certainly in the spirit of the early Irish monks and some version of it could have been familiar to Patrick or others of his day. Its form and style reflects a pre-Christian tradition of invocation and blessing. Known as the Lorica, or Breastplate, it is a prayer "for the protection of body and soul."

> For my shield this day I call:
> A mighty power:
> The Holy Trinity!
> Affirming threeness,
> Confessing oneness,
> In the making of all
> Through love. . . .

> For my shield this day I call:
> strong power of the seraphim,
> with angels obeying,
> and archangels attending,
> in the glorious company
> of the holy and risen ones. . . .

> For my shield this day I call:
> Heaven's might,
> Sun's brightness,
> Moon's whiteness,
> Fire's glory,
> Lightning's swiftness,
> Wind's wildness,
> Ocean's depth,

Earth's solidity,
Rock's mobility.

This day I call to me:
  God's strength to direct me,
  God's power to sustain me,
  God's wisdom to guide me,
  God's vision to light me,
  God's ear to my hearing,
  God's word to my speaking,
  God's hand to uphold me,
  God's pathway before me. . . .

Be Christ this day my strong protector. . . .
  Christ beside me, Christ before me;
  Christ behind me, Christ within me;
  Christ beneath me, Christ above me;
  Christ to the right of me, Christ to the left of me;
  Christ in my lying, my sitting, my rising;
  Christ in heart of all who know me,
  Christ on tongue of all who meet me,
  Christ in eye of all who see me,
  Christ in ear of all who hear me.[8]

It is important to note that the women and men repeating this invocation with passion and expectation as they traveled the Irish countryside were not praying to a deity removed from the world. There are no intermediaries here. The appeal to the angelic kingdom and to the powers of nature is as direct and immediate as the asking for protection and blessing from the Creator. Likewise, the invocation of Christ reveals the Celtic emphasis not primarily on the redemptive, intercessory work of Christ, but on the mystical Body in which all life is held in love and blessing. In this vision of Christ in everybody (and in everything), the whole of creation becomes luminous.[9]

Perhaps the most sophisticated interpretation of Celtic Christianity's green theology is found in the work of John Scotus Eriugena, the brilliant ninth-century Irish scholar who some say may have been the most original of the great Scholastic thinkers of the Middle Ages. In his extensive work, *On the Division of Nature,* he argued that all creation "in all its wonderful diversity is a living theophany, a manifestation of the Word."[10] Nature and Scripture were for him the two shoes of Christ. "We should not understand God and the creatures as two things removed from one another, but as one and the same thing. For the creature subsists in God, and God is created in the creature in a wonderful and ineffable way, making himself manifest, invisible making himself visible."[11] The immanent nature of God, he believed, is fully manifest only when God is also recognized as transcendent to the created order, as the source and sustainer, the one from whom all life flows and into which all life returns. Eriugena, nonetheless, was condemned as pantheist and heretical by the medieval church. His influence, however, is clearly evident in the mystics, particularly in the work of Saint Francis, Meister Eckhart, and Hildegard of Bingen.

Celtic Christianity developed in its own unique pattern for about a thousand years before falling under the dominance of Roman orthodoxy. Its life-celebrating spirit and hopeful perspective on human nature were in time replaced by the Augustinian pessimism that has, since the medieval period, characterized so much of both Catholic and Reformed Christianity. Its high regard for nature, evident in both a "unique passion for the wild and elemental—and in a gentle human love for all creation, fellow creatures all with God,"[12] was lost as Christianity focused attention wholly on the salvation of the human soul. It is interesting to reflect on how differently Western culture might have developed, and what the consequences would have been for the environment, if the creation-affirming spirituality of Celtic Christianity had remained accessible as a guiding source of wisdom and direction.

Irish Christianity is of course not the only buried tradition of ecological responsibility to which we can turn for help in meeting the present crisis. To an unprecedented degree today we have access to the wisdom of the world's religious traditions as well as the ancient Earth-oriented spirituality of indigenous peoples. These rich streams of human experience and inspiration are now being tapped as people within and outside conventional religious institutions work to recover an alternative to the human-centered story that has dominated Western Christianity and to articulate a needed environmental theology. There is a new and lively conversation under way in many religious institutions and denominations as theology is reexamined in light of our new knowledge about the Earth and its living systems. New doctrinal statements are being crafted and adopted regarding Earth ethics and eco-justice. As these make their way into liturgy and congregational life, the Church may have a new opportunity to become a dynamic and effective voice on behalf of the Earth.

Yet, we have a very long way to go. The ethics and behaviors generated by the "old story" do not easily give way to the new. Trends are not necessarily destiny, we know, but nonetheless, past decisions and choices cast their long shadow over the future. The decades ahead will not be easy for a great many people, nor for many species. No doubt there will be those who vehemently maintain destructive patterns of greed and the continuing oppression of other people, most of them poor, on which overconsumption by the few depends. The anticipated increase in the world's population means further pillage of the natural world as the struggle to survive, particularly in the developing nations, justifies the continuing abuse of nature.

Something else, hopeful and strong, may also happen, for there is in humankind an undeniable capacity to meet great crises with tremendous creativity and hope. The rise of a new, innovative spirit is already evident as concerned people turn hearts and minds, ingenuity and skill, time and money, into the healing and restoration of the natural world and to meeting the legitimate needs of *every* species for whom the Earth is home. We must count on unpredictable and extraordinary breakthroughs in the years ahead as we come to grips with the truth that there can be no long-term health and happiness for the human family unless it is in consort with the health and generativity of the natural world.

So, I think it all comes down to how each of us grapples with the soul-troubling questions of our day. What we choose to believe will determine in unprecedented ways what life will be like for those coming after us who, after all, are our own children and theirs. They will surely call us to account.

In the next years, it will be easy to try to walk away from the questions. It will be tempting to succumb to the illusion of simple answers and go for short-run measures that postpone the inevitable *metanoia,* the turning around, the changing of heart and mind necessary if we are to assure a viable future for coming generations.

But well-packed questions don't let you walk away. They disturb the bones. You can't put them down, for they work at that place in you that has to do with the bedrock meaning of your life, your hopes, your deepest beliefs, what you most love, and what legacy you want to leave for the future.

I think we will make it. I think there are enough of us who will go with the Irish, so to speak. I think we will choose to believe that the well-packed questions of our in-between moment in history are gifts. We will welcome them. We will go wherever they take us. We will expect them to reveal their wisdom—and we will do whatever we must to make sure that they grow at last to good answers.

✦ 2 ✦

Into the Future

by THOMAS BERRY

Since the appearance of *Silent Spring* by Rachel Carson in 1962 we have been reflecting on the tragic consequences of the plundering industrial society that we have brought into existence during these past few centuries. That we should have caused such damage to the entire functioning of the planet Earth in all its major biosystems is obviously the consequence of a deep cultural pathology.

Just as clearly there is need for a deep cultural therapy if we are to proceed into the future with some assurance that we will not continue in this pathology or lapse into the same pathology at a later date. We still do not have such a critique of the past or a therapy for the present. Yet even without such evaluation of our present situation we must proceed with the task of creating a viable future for ourselves and for the entire planetary process.

The two things needed to guide our judgment and to sustain the psychic energies required for the task are a certain terror at what is happening at present, and a fascination with the future that is available to us if only we respond creatively to the urgencies of the present.

I am concerned in this chapter with the second of these requirements. I wish especially to outline the conditions for entering onto a future that will lead to that wonderful fulfillment for which the entire planet as well as ourselves seems to be destined.

The first condition for achieving this objective is to realize that the universe is a communion of subjects, not a collection of objects.

The devastation of the planet can be seen as a direct consequence of a loss of this capacity for human presence to the nonhuman world. This reached its most decisive moment in the seventeenth-century proposal of René Descartes that the universe is composed simply of "mind and mechanism." In this single stroke he, in a sense, killed the planet and all its living creatures with the exception of the human.

The thousandfold voices of the natural world suddenly became inaudible to the human. The mountains and rivers and the wind and the sea all became mute insofar as humans were concerned. The forests were no longer the abode of an infinite number of spirit presences but were simply so many board feet of timber to be "harvested" as objects to be used for human benefit. Animals were no longer the companions of humans in the single community of existence. They were denied not only their inherent dignity, but even their rights to habitat.

As we recover our awareness of the universe as a communion of subjects a new interior experience awakens within the human. The barriers disappear. An enlargement of soul takes place. The excitement evoked by all natural phenomena is renewed. Dawn and sunset are once again transforming experiences as are all the sights and sounds and scents and tastes and the feel of the natural world about us, the surging sea, the sound of the wind, the brooding forests. All this could be continued in a never-ending listing of the experiences that take place constantly throughout the planet, experiences that have been lost to large segments of the human community in recent centuries—not because the phenomena do not surround us constantly, but that we have become autistic, as though large segments of the human mind have become paralyzed. It is no wonder that humans have devastated the planet so extensively. It was only a collection of objects to be used.

Associated with this attitude is the loss of realization that the planet Earth is a onetime endowment. It came into being at a moment that will never occur again. It was given a structure and a quantum of energy for its self-shaping processes whereby it could bring forth all those remarkable geological formations and all those magnificent modes of life expression that we see about us. The Earth was caught up in an inner dynamism that is overwhelming in its impact on human consciousness. These energies have been functioning throughout these past millennia with remarkable genius in a sequence of transformations on this planet that will never take place again. The quantum of energy needed has been expended. Species that we wantonly extinguish will never appear again. The quantum of energy involved in their historical existence has been expended.

There does exist at present a quantum of energy available for a creative movement from the terminal Cenozoic era to the emergent Ecozoic. Yet it will be available only for a brief period of time. Such transformation moments arise in times of crisis that need resolution immediately. So with the present the time for action is passing. The devastation increases. Yet the time is limited. The Great Work remains to be done. This is not a situation that can be remedied by trivial or painless means. A largeness of vision and a supreme dedication are needed.

Our only hope for such a renewal is our awakening to the realization that the Earth is primary and that humans are derivative. That this relation should be so obvious and yet so consistently violated is beyond all understanding. This primacy of the Earth community applies to every mode of human activity: economics, education, law, medicine, religion. The human is a subsystem of the Earth system. The primary concern in every phase of human activity must be to preserve the integrity of the Earth system. Only then can the subsystems function with any efficacy. Yet no phase of human activity is so directly violated as this relation of the human to the Earth.

In the realm of jurisprudence, the English Common Law tradition that has claimed such superiority in its conceptions of the human and the dignity of the human, has little sense of the larger governing principles of the universe or of the planet. This tradition lays great emphasis on the rights of humans. In this context the nonhuman world has become property to be used by the human. A governance and a jurisprudence founded in the supremacy of the already-existing Earth governance is needed. An interspecies jurisprudence is needed. The primary community is not the human community but the Earth community. The primary obligations are to the success of this larger community.

Especially in religion the human depends on the natural system. For it is the wonder and majesty of the universe that evokes the sense of the divine and the sensitivity to the sacred. For the universe is a mysterious reality. We can know only the marginal aspects of how the universe or the Earth functions. Once the divine is perceived through written Scriptures there is then a tendency to exclude the evidences of the natural world of things, for these, it is thought, do not communicate the sense of the sacred except in some minor way. Yet we can never replace our need for a resplendent natural world if we are to respond effectively to the exaltation of the divine or our sense of the sacred.

Since the discovery of the universe as an evolutionary process there is the need to establish a new sense of the revelatory experience. That this new mode of experiencing the universe carries with it a new modality in the manifestation of the ultimate mysteries of the universe implies that future generations will need to be religious within this context. Our traditional Scriptures will probably not be effective in awakening future generations to a sense of the sacred as they have done in past generations. This will involve a serious process of adaptation, a new awakening to the divine not only through the awesome qualities of the universe as experienced immediately, but also through the immense story of the universe and its long series of transformations.

We also need to establish rituals for celebrating these transformation moments that have enabled the universe and the planet Earth to develop over the past many years. This would involve celebrating the primordial moment of emergence of the universe and such other transformation moments as the supernova collapse of the first generation of stars whereby the ninety-some elements needed for life and consciousness came into existence. We should especially celebrate that star out of which our own solar system was born and the various life forms of Earth became possible.

The discovery of sexual reproduction upon which the evolutionary process depends so directly, the discovery of photosynthesis, of respiration, the emergence of life out of the sea and its venturing onto the land, the appearance of the first trees, the first flowering plants, the transition to the Cenozoic period, the emergence of the human—all these are sacred moments. To celebrate these occasions would renew our sense of the sacred character of the universe and of the planet Earth.

Another condition for entering a viable relationship of the human with the Earth community is a realization that the planet Earth will never again function in the future in the manner that it has functioned in the past. A decisive transformation has taken place, for whereas the human had nothing to say in the emergent period of the universe prior to the present, in the future the human will be involved in almost everything that happens. We have passed over a threshold. While we cannot make a blade of grass, there is liable not to be a blade of grass in the future unless it is accepted, protected, and fostered by the human. Sometimes, too, there is a healing that can be brought about by human assistance.

Just now our modern world with its scientific technologies, its industrial processes, and its commercial establishments functions with amazing arrogance in our human attitude toward the natural world. The assumption is that the human is the supreme reality and that every other being is available for exploitation in the service of the human. The supreme law of economics is to take as much as possible of the Earth's resources to be processed, passed through the consumer economy as quickly as possible, and then deposited as residue on the waste heap. The greater amount of natural resources consumed in this manner, the greater the Gross Domestic Product or the Gross Human Product, the more successful the human enterprise is thought to be, although the final consequence of such an economic program is to turn the entire planet into a wasteland. Any sense of the sacred, any restraints in favor of the inner coherence and resplendence of the natural world, these are thought of as the expression of an unendurable romanticism.

Yet the planet now exists in a more intricate relation with the human than ever before. The very devastation wrought by the human has brought about a new type of violence in human-Earth relationships. Yet this apparent control by the human does not imply that the human can, as it were, run the planet or bring the planet into any context that the human wishes. The human can bring about extinction on a broad scale, but it cannot bring about life through its own power. It can only assist in some limited way in evoking life through the processes inherent in the Earth itself.

The ultimate goal of any renewal process must be to establish a "mutually enhancing mode of human presence on the Earth." While this mutual enhancement can be achieved only within limits, since the human, as every other being, in some manner places stress upon the larger process, it is something that can make the gains and the losses more proportional and more acceptable within the larger context of the planetary community.

What can be hoped for is a sense of the human joining in the larger liturgy of the universe itself. The very cosmological patterns of universe-functioning that were established in much earlier times can be considered as a primordial liturgy. This liturgy inherent in the ancient mystique of the Earth and its functioning might be established once again—this time, however, not simply in the traditional sequence of seasonal renewal, but also in the sequence of irreversible transformations that can now be identified as the larger story of the planetary process.

This story of the universe now becomes the basic context for education. This comprehensive context includes all education, from the earliest period of schooling through to professional schools. The story of the universe expresses a functional cosmology that needs to be taught at every level of training. To be educated is to know the story and the human role in the story. Through this story we come to know the manner whereby we ourselves came into being and the role that we should be fulfilling in the story. Because our capacity to tell this story in its full dimensions in space and in its sequence of transformations in time is only recently attained, we are only now beginning to understand its significance.

Through this story we can now guide our way through this transition phase of our history, from the terminal Cenozoic into the emerging Ecozoic. This emergent phase of Earth history can be defined as that period when humans would be present to the Earth in a mutually enhancing manner. This story evokes not only the guidance but also the psychic energy needed to carry out the sequence of transformations that is now required of us as we move into the future.

Throughout its vast extent in space and its long sequence of transformations in time the universe constitutes a single, multiform, sequential, celebratory event. Every being in the universe is intimately present to and influencing every other being in the universe. Every being contributes to the magnificence of the whole. Because the universe is the only self-referent mode of being in the phenomenal world it constitutes the norm of all reality and value. The universe is the only text without context. Every particular mode of being is universe-referent and its meaning is established only within this comprehensive setting. This is the reason why this story of the universe, and especially of the planet Earth, is so all-important. Through our understanding of this story our own role in the story is revealed. In this revelation lies our way into the future.

✦ *3* ✦

Practicing the Presence
by JOANNA MACY

Our culture wants us enclosed in a very tight compartment of time, increasingly cutting us off from past and future. But there is a different time into which we can enter. We can enter into *deep time* where we can feel the presence and the companionship of the beings of the past and the beings of the future. They are with us. The future beings are present in you and me. Take this as a blessing. Accept their companionship. Feel the influx of their knowing and their caring and their energy. Feel yourself informed by their love of this planet that they tended for so many millennia. Feel yourself lifted by their desire to be born on this planet and to have their turn to care for it. And draw from their gifts like so much money in the bank.

We are not here just on our own. We are here for them, too. We can enlist their support, as we, the ones alive now, who are standing at this brink of time, cast our votes, organize, and make a difference now.

In this extraordinary time, as we practice the presence of our unseen companions, those of the past and those of the future, let us also remember the presence of those here with us now: the presence of the old growth forests, the presence of the seals and otters, of the sea gulls whose wings are sealed with oil from an oil spill and cannot fly. Practice the presence of our Ukranian brothers and sisters, farmers on a radioactive soil, heirs of Chernobyl, of our African brothers and sisters migrating across scorched land, decimated by AIDS, of our brothers and sisters who are downwind from the Nevada test site, and of South Sea islanders who are living with the aftermath of our nuclear tests, of families in the Middle East, uprooted by the hostility bred by our greed for oil. These unseen companions are also at our side, unseen companions for whom we can speak. Let them share with us their dignity and endurance. Let them keep us to the mark.

Let all these then be our community, so that whether our efforts to heal our world succeed or fail, we will know we have done our part in awakening the power of our love. This in itself, is enough.

·4·

The Joining of Human, Earth, and Spirit

by DANIEL MARTIN

> The human community and the natural world will go into
> the future as a single sacred community or we will both
> perish in the desert.
>
> —*Thomas Berry*[1]

The basic problem, the essential cause of our present world crisis, is that we humans do not feel at home. We do not feel that *we belong* with the rest of creation; not the way the trees and the rivers do; not like the birds and the animals. We feel, rather, that we're somehow different, maybe even introduced into this world from someplace else, souls from another realm who are passing through an alien and unfriendly land. The consequence is that in our efforts to protect ourselves we have separated from the rest of this world and the separation has, all too often, translated into defensive arrogance that has resulted in the destruction of our world. In the end, of course, this is also our own destruction.

The solution to our predicament turns on a sense of belonging: the re-joining of humankind and the Earth in a mutually enriching relationship.

Brian Friel's play *Dancing at Lughnasa,* which has been a success on both sides of the Atlantic, is about two responses to a world that is beginning to collapse, experienced in very concrete fashion in Ireland in 1936. It is the story of five sisters—all unmarried, one with a son, living in a closed, conservative community, and their brother, a missionary priest, who is something of a local hero through his efforts in Africa and who has just come home. However, instead of coming back to take his heroic place, and thereby also adding to the sisters' standing in the community, he has returned converted to another way of looking at life, to strangely "pagan" attitudes and values.

Naturally, the lives of the sisters are disrupted. All their assumptions are challenged, about religion and tradition, certainly, but also about themselves and the lives they lead. The oldest sister expresses it for the rest:

> You work hard at your job. You try to keep the home together. You perform your duties as best you can—because you believe in responsibilities and obligations and good order. And then suddenly, suddenly you realize that hair cracks are appearing everywhere; that control is slipping away; that the whole thing is so fragile it can't be held together much longer.[2]

The words cannot fail to touch us today, for we can all resonate with the feeling, whether we have known it in the form of unemployment or failure of some sort, or sickness or death. It is the collapse of what we have come to know as our world and it is the frantic struggle to hold on to some semblance of control.

In the background to the play, there is the Celtic (pagan) celebration of Lughnasa, the feast of abundance and extravagance, a time of wildness and freedom. Lughnasa, in fact, is the symbol of the life that we do not control, the chaos that we try to keep at bay by our obviously futile efforts to hold it all together, but which is always lurking just behind the next bend. Occasionally, the spirit of Lughnasa breaks through the sisters' growing anxiety, at one stage drawing them into a wild, carefree dance, a kind of ecstasy that transports them beyond their fearful attempts to "hold it all together."

At the end of the play when everything has fallen apart, it is suggested that there is actually another way of living in the face of change or collapse. It is the way of the "dance," the way of participation, the way of working with things, rather than the way of control. It is a way based on the realization that we really do belong, that we are part of the life we struggle so hard against; that this life that has created us and continues to hold us in existence will also be the source of our joy if we can learn to let go of our fear and move within its rhythms, respond to its laws that are, in fact, already written on our hearts.

Dance is a metaphor for the world and its unfolding. It is a symbol for the restless movement of the cosmos as it brings things together in partnership and eases them apart again for new relationships. And it is also our "way," our "Tao": the wisdom that knows how to move with this restlessness, and to see our own restlessness, not as a problem, but an expression of, and contributing component to, the infinite cosmic dance.

My childhood experience of life was much closer to this wisdom. Born of Celtic blood, raised on stories of magical places and healers, and a hardly discernible veil between this world and the "other world," I would know this kind of experience regularly in the fields and hills where I grew up, watching lapwings and curlews protect their nests against marauding neighbors, which included young boys like myself. Here I belonged, here I was at home. In this world everything was connected; Earth and Spirit went hand in hand, sprung from the one source, serving and feeding each other.

I recall an experience that captures this continuum. I was about thirteen years old and, out of curiosity, had joined a couple of uncles on a trip to the local Trappist monastery where they went occasionally for a retreat. We arrived at the place, an old Georgian building, in the late summer evening when the monks had already finished their evening prayers and were settling down for the customary early night. Our room overlooked the monastery fields that were bathed in the long, soft light of sunset. I can remember going over to the window with the milk and cookies—traditional welcome food—to check out the scene and what promised to be, for a young boy, a rather unexciting weekend.

As I looked out, I saw a lone monk, in black-and-white habit, standing under a sycamore tree, in a field that sloped gently down to the river, in apparent contemplation of the setting sun. At that point something happened that has remained with me ever since. Nothing changed, or rather, it all changed. Everything was suddenly heightened and stood out in sharp relief: the monk, the tree, the field, the river, the sun, and the watching boy all suffused with some kind of light that joined them together: a fire with many flames. It was like seeing for the first time, or being awakened from a deep sleep into a sun-filled room.

It was like the web that indigenous people speak about, the web that binds things together, that we cannot touch in any place without affecting all the rest of it. It is the way things really are, these people say, which we, in the modern world, unfortunately, have lost the ability to see.

That experience was a special gift for me. It burned itself on my soul as somehow the measure of all truth. This, I knew ever after, is how things are. In time, I came to realize that this was what religion was about also at some level, even if it too, like the rest of our world, had lost the ability to see.

So, here, I would suggest, is the crux of the matter: how to begin to see things as they truly are; how to touch the fire of a moment or a place; how to experience oneself as intimately connected to the web. If we were to see things in this way, we would know that we belong, that this is our home. And we would know how to dance. Imagine a world built on this kind of experience: imagine a world in tune with the rhythms of this dance.

But how do we touch the fire? How see the web? How deal with the fear that we experience as "cosmic orphans" who do not belong? How deal with the rage that causes us not only to manipulate and control but also to destroy anything that would remind us of our situation?

The native people of Australia also say it is fear that makes us blind, fear that turns into rage against our helpless finitude. For the Aborigines, though, it is an extremely concrete fear, having to do with basic survival: "Anyone who does not know how to find food and feed himself is always frightened inside like a little child who has lost his mother, and with that fear the vision of the spirit world departs."[3]

It is a fear that goes all the way back to our first efforts to move beyond the hunter-gatherer relationship of give and take, to a world that depends on our ingenuity and skill to make and manipulate in order to survive. It was the activities of agriculture and the religions they gave birth to, that fostered the separation of humans from the

Earth, by turning human attention away from the deeper, symbolic dimensions of life toward the physical manipulation of the material world. In time this became the only means of survival.

"In time" refers to the long history of ideas and events that shaped and developed the sophisticated forms our survival techniques took, and the self-understanding that they engendered. This history reveals two tendencies: one is the humanist—"the city" is its symbol; the other is the environmentalist.

The humanist tradition is, naturally, human-centered, representing our attempts to defend ourselves against the wilderness and its chaos, and create order and meaning. It is the history of an increasing ability to manipulate, in the form of agriculture, and later, science and technology. It is the history of the city where the human reigns supreme, keeping at bay the threat of chaos, making forays into the unknown of the wilderness, only to retreat to the safety of the city ramparts. It is the history of what Lewis Mumford has called the "illusion of limited control."

However, the alternative, the environmentalist tendency, as articulated in its more recent form, can be similarly ineffective. This approach attempts to redefine the human, either by relegation to a non-distinctive place in the ranks of all species—or to the level of villain, the blight of all other forms of life—or by inflation to some kind of steward on whom the world depends for survival. "To care for the Earth" has become a common catchphrase for this approach, though it begs the question as to who cares for whom.

Neither category has worked because neither one is complete. They ignore the basic discontinuity that characterizes our relationship with the rest of nature. In fact, we are both connected to and, at the same time, separate from the Earth, a relationship that, Robert Harrison notes in *Forests*, is captured by the notion of *logos*, a term that implies both connectedness and separation. It is the power that gives shape to things. It is what Gregory Bateson has called the "pattern that connects" and what the Christian world has identified as the Cosmic Christ who forms creation. We share this "logos."[4]

Oikos (eco-), which means "home" in Greek, is the other part of the word *ecology*. It completes the picture of our relationship with the world as one of connectedness *and* separation. We are born of the Earth, but we are constantly reaching for the stars; we are part of the cosmos but also a reflection of its infinite restlessness: it is, in fact, our particular way of belonging. But this kind of self-understanding requires a basic shift in our present distorted worldview. We need a new context, a new story of life and how we fit into it.

Context has to do with story: the story of life's origins and the roles that it offers to each player in the drama. The Australian Aboriginal story clearly determined how people fit into the larger context of things. First there is the Dream that is the ground of all being, the Source from which all differentiation arises. In the beginning was the Dreaming, they would say.

The world was created by the Ancestors—the gods, the first children of the Dream—through their hunting, fighting, and playing. Their adventures—their dreams—created the mountains and lakes, the trees, the birds and the animals, even the humans. Everything, in other words, came from the same source, as the external manifestation of the dreams of the Ancestors. Everything, therefore, is an expression of the first Dream.

This "other world" of the Dream is reached through dream memories that are inscribed eternally in the world around us—in the plants and animals, in the land itself. Song is the link, the sound, the vibratory pattern, that each thing emits as its own name: the "name" that the Ancestors gave it, in establishing it in existence, in singing it into life. So the Aborigines listen to the land and its creatures in order to hear the songs and remember the names that tell them of the original song. And that is their role, their function in the greater scheme of things. When they do this, everything else falls into place. When they do not, there is chaos.

The land, then, is inherently sacred to them, for it carries the echoes of the original Dream. Their special calling is to preserve the land in its original form, for to destroy it would be to destroy life itself. Human beings, therefore, influence the world, far beyond our individual lives. When we are out of tune with life, when our relationships among ourselves or with the land are distorted, the world itself is in grave danger.

I heard many of the same themes in Africa where I lived for about ten years in the ambivalent world of the "postmodern missionary," caught between two ages—the colonial and the so-called independent—unsure of the future. Laurens Van der Post, who has written extensively about Africa, describes the Bushman of the Kalahari in terms that echo the Aboriginal sense of the symbolic. The essence of their being, says Van der Post, was a sense of belonging: they belonged not only to themselves, but to nature, the Earth, the universe itself. For the Bushman, story was what held life together: the story of the universe echoed in the world around. A story is the wind, the sun, the mountain. As long as they could hear the sound of the sun and the stars—could hear their song—and could move (dance) to their music, all was well in the world; but when the sound ceased, tragedy fell upon them. In fact, like all our ancestors in this faith of belonging, the Bushman, when they would dance to the moon and the stars, move to the rhythms of the seasons, could live with strength and meaning, and die with tranquility, without complaint or regret.[5]

This ancient context, which is echoed in many other indigenous cultures, is emerging now in our own, ironically from within the world of science. Though it is probably somewhat extreme to categorize science as a spiritless perspective, in its modern form it has fostered, as well as built itself on, a fundamental materialism. However, a transformation has begun in this traditionally dichotomized world that is making science a new prophet, the herald of a rediscovered Earth-spirit continuum.

Some fundamental questions capture the picture. Where do we come from? A millionth of a second slower or faster and life as we know it could not have evolved. Who are we? Born of Earth and water that are themselves the gifts of the stars in their dying process, we are the universe come to consciousness. Where are we? With our growing ability to manipulate the physical universe, we have brought ourselves and much of life to the edge of extinction. What shall we do? What has the universe done in the past in the face of imminent disaster? What miraculous breakthrough will it bring about this time? We would be well advised to listen, to pay attention, to tap into the creative energies that are present in a special way at this time of collapse and rebirth. For while the world, as it has come to be in the last sixty-five million years of the Cenozoic era, is clearly passing away, a new era is being born, the Ecozoic era that we hope will include us.

Indigenous people speak about going back to the original instructions that were given to us as human beings, that is in our genetic coding, in a sense. The original story—like the original event—has its own power to revitalize. Today, scientific evidence offers a common creation story that links us to the cosmos in new empirically based realization. As this realization translates into personal stories, it will become the mythic context that inspires and directs us into a new era.

But it is not enough to know these things, we first have to experience them in our lives. Only experience initiates change. Experience grabs us, takes us out of ourselves and our prejudices. Understanding and knowledge fill out the experience so that we begin to think and decide differently. Of course, experience itself is already preformed or prejudiced by our background. We hear and see only what we are able to, and therein lies the problem. We have become what Thomas Berry has called the "autistic generation," the people who do not hear or see: nothing gets in, and nothing gets out. So how do we break through this barrier and break out of the sophisticated denial mechanisms that we have developed over the years of illusory success?

Essentially there are two things that bring about real change in us: one is when we are grasped by something or someone, when we fall in love, for example. The other, ironically, is fear, the very thing that has caused our crisis in the first place. Both take us out of ourselves and cause the perspective to shift radically so that we suddenly see things in a new way, as I did that day in the monastery.

To say that we change only when we have to is very much a truism in regard to normal behavior. But change also threatens us, as we noted earlier, stirs up the fundamental fear of annihilation. It can even paralyze us into passivity so that we accept what we consider to be inevitable. The kind of fear that gets us moving, on the other hand, is what economist, Herman Daly describes as an "optimal disaster," one that is sufficient to get home the message without wiping us out. A sort of cosmic nudge.

One aspect of this kind of fear is that it is not produced by knowledge in the narrow sense of information. All the education in the world will not change people, as Aldo Leopold, the marvelous naturalist of Sand County fame, insisted. I am reminded of the great *Titanic* that was built in my own home town of Belfast, the epitome of modern technology. The *Titanic*, it was discovered later, had received at least seven warnings of imminent danger, but had simply ignored them, for reasons we can probably guess, since they are the kinds of reasons we use ourselves in our own *"Titanic* situations." Fear comes through the senses, a primal experience of threat that is felt rather than understood, that leaves little room for rationalization. If we are able to receive it, it can be the gift of "optimal disaster" that causes us to change what we are doing. Fear of this nature awakens us, empowers us, in fact, with its adrenaline-supporting surge.

It is the same with the more positive form of "being grasped"— falling in love. People in love have not reasoned themselves into being in love. But here also a certain sensitivity, and ability to hear and see, is required. Our awakening to things as they are is through a process of resensitizing our dulled senses. In this way we can begin to take back our lives from the autism of our own making. There are two aspects of this resensitizing process.

One is the simple practice of being there, what we might call *real presence*. Thich Nhat Hanh, a Zen Buddhist monk, teaches this art of "mindfulness" in activities as mundane as washing dishes. He describes how we must feel the water and the soap, the shape of the dishes and the weight of the pots, without rushing ahead to have dessert, for example, the pleasure of which will be lessened if we do not really stay first with the task at hand.[6]

The implication is clear: we are seldom really present to what we are doing, our mind being divided among the many concerns that demand our attention. Our separation is not simply physical, it is also in our minds. The habit of not being present prevents us from enjoying anything fully, while the practice of this "unmindfulness" deepens our pathology. Part of reconnecting with the world, part of fostering the experience of belonging, is this "mind-changing" practice of simply being present.

Wendell Berry, a poet-farmer from Kentucky, examines another dimension of real presence: the area of food. We have allowed the basic and personal act of eating that could be an intimate communion with the Earth to become an industrial transaction between ourselves and the factory-supermarket complex. In this transaction, food, the fruit of the Earth, is fertilized and sprayed with chemicals, treated for preservation, pounded, processed, colored, and coated in costly packaging, so that what reaches us bears little relation to the original expression of Earth life that came out of the ground.[7]

There is, moreover, the added dimension of the politics and economics that turns this transaction into the abuse of Third World land and its peoples through a free-market system that fosters the world of cash crops and cheap labor; that prevents countries, rich in food potential, from feeding their own people. Here again, we need to take back our lives, by learning how to participate in this most basic human function: grow some food, even in a window box, buy sensitively, cook for ourselves, educate ourselves about the politics of food, join a cooperative. For the way we eat, actually determines the way the world gets used.

The same thing applies to other basic functions, like water use, or waste treatment, including our own sewage. Part of belonging to the Earth clearly has to do with the ability to perform the basic functions of survival, like finding food and shelter. The intimate relationship indigenous peoples have with Mother Earth, and that we tend to romanticize as abstract feeling, is an extremely concrete expression of realized interdependence. They know the qualities of each tree and plant, where to find water, and how to create basic shelter. In this way they are truly children of a generous and abundant mother.

Real presence also has to be about learning to relate in a new way to all the things around us: the mountains, rivers, trees, plants, and animals that the prevailing worldview tells us are either dead matter or of a lesser nature, and simply there for our use. Thomas Berry speaks of "listening to the voices" of the trees, the mountains, the moon and the stars, the birds and the animals. Once again, in this apparently simplistic suggestion, there lies a wisdom, now rediscovered by modern science but known by our ancestors who listened for the sound of the sun and the mountain, who could hear the song of each thing, and know how to relate appropriately.

Aboriginal cosmology explained that the Dreamtime Ancestors called each thing into being by giving it its own vibratory pattern, its own name, as it were. Their legend is echoed in the Judeo-Christian tradition that tells us how the first humans gave names to the creatures. Today, science speaks of the interiority of each organism, its own integral form of energy that gives it autonomy and identity. "Listening to the voices" takes on new significance that should encourage us to respect the silence that allows us to begin to hear again the voices of the world we share.

Of course, this world speaks also in spectacular fashion, through its own seasonal changes. In sound and color, it calls to us to be aware, to simply see and hear. Alice Walker's book *The Color Purple* describes how "God is forever trying to attract our attention to her beauty and gets really annoyed if we walk past a field of purple flowers and just don't notice."[8] Learning to notice requires the attention to detail that one finds in the excitement of the naturalist or the wonder of a child. It is the sense of awe.

Real presence is to begin to see and hear again. It is to take back one's life from the forces of illusion, the creations of fear. It is to begin to live again—deliberately, as Thoreau would say—with the accuracy, the attention to detail that characterized the world of the Bushman; with the sensitivity that is born of participation in the basic functions of living; with the mindfulness that is able to be simply present; and with the awe that never trivializes. Without recovering this desensitized part of our own being, we will not be able to create and sustain a vision on which a life of meaning depends.

The second aspect of the re-sensitizing process is remembering—stirring that part of ourselves that is fundamentally connected to the web. In other words, at some long-lost level of ourselves we know what is true, we know who we are: we have simply forgotten. But we have vast stores of wisdom available to help us overcome our amnesia.

The very process of resensitizing offers its own archival treasures. Food, water, breath, all carry their own memory banks, providing us not simply with energy-nourishment, but also with information that tells us who we are, touching directly the deep memory in us. The elaboration of this direct experience in words and concepts, however, is also important to bring our awareness to a new level of completeness.

This kind of elaboration is found in the human libraries of Scriptures, ritual, literature, folk tales, dance, and music. These are the records of our attempts to articulate the experience of real presence and the world that it reveals. In the light of a new context, these ancient intuitions come to life again: under the light of a common, cosmic, creation story, insights, long since stultified, and rendered powerless by insistent literalism, are liberated to reveal their magic, the magic that, in turn, releases us into new realization. Thus the "burning bush" that Moses encountered becomes a reminder that the ground we are standing on is already holy ground. In a similar way the words "This is my body" reveal a cosmic realization of oneness while the religious question, "Who is my neighbor?" takes on significance far beyond our human-protecting world.

The insights of the mystics are often more direct, because they have been freer of the cultural biases that shaped our scriptural interpretations. Thus, we read with immediate comprehension in Eckhart, that "every creature is a book about God," or, in Julian of Norwich, that "everything has being because of God's love." The poets, too, are often mystics who have reached deep into that part of their individual lives where they are one with everything; who reach also into the future in shamanic service to the larger community, to anticipate, as it were, the shape of things to come.

In a similar way, we all share something of the shamanic adventure through ritual, through word and gesture, shaped and honed by generations of experience. My own experience with ritual of many varieties, both cultural and denominational, suggests to me that basically rituals are all attempts, not only to express the inexpressible, but to enter into it. Gerard Manley Hopkins refers to the many landscapes of the one "inscape" where we meet the one mystery that grounds all life. Perhaps this is why contemplatives who try to share this inscape often understand one another, while theologians, whose focus is the many landscapes, seldom do so.

But there are other sources of remembering closer to home and less formal, such as the treasures to be found in folk tradition. The Brothers Grimm were clearly aware of how wisdom—revelation of the truth of things—was communicated through the stories people told one another around their hearths, the stories that were the storehouses of oral tradition. The same memories are discernible in folk music and dance. In dance, in a particular way, the rhythms of the Earth, the movements of the stars, and the vibrations—the voices—of the plants and the animals, are felt in body and spirit.

Today there is a marked revival of these wonderful forms of community remembering that nourish and rejuvenate as well as any formal liturgy. For all these rituals, each in its own way and at its own particular level, are stimulants of the deep memory that will enable us to recover from our cosmic amnesia.

Finally, there is the personal store that each one of us carries, and that is often accessed by an association that wings us back to the original experience. Marcel Proust, in his work on *temps perdu* (things in the past) spoke of the effect of a smell or (in his case) the taste of a little cake, and its power to recover—to bring right into the present—an experience from the past. It is as if memories actually remained in existence somewhere, waiting only for the magic word (or smell) to release them.

It is when these insights of tradition that stir the "deep memory" meet with a world experienced by senses that have been revitalized that something quite new is born: a new revelation of the truth, a new experience of how things truly are, a real presence in the moment. This is what the Aborigines describe as seeing the web of life; this is what the mystics describe as the "fullness of joy that is felt in seeing God in everything." It is what I experienced with the monk, the river, and the tree. It is what we have all experienced, however fleetingly, in those moments when life opens and reveals itself.

At such times we are no longer unsure of who we are or how we fit in. Our role is determined by a new appreciation of how things really are. This is being grasped by the mysterious purposes of the universe, falling in love in an infinite way. Then we belong and the world becomes our home once again. This experience alone is the foundation on which a new world can be built. Anything less is about rearranging the pieces of an old one.

This primary experience, this process of change and growth, needs to be taken a step further. It has to move through the stages of understanding and reflection, to articulation, and then to decision and action. It needs, in fact, to be articulated as principles that capture the spirit of the world that is anticipated.

There is a time for such proclamation. Two hundred years ago, Thomas Jefferson realized that it was necessary to proclaim the principles of a world that needed to be helped into birth. He saw that already certain things were "self-evident." Today, the things that are becoming self-evident—the interconnectedness of life, the sacredness of all creatures, the primacy of the Earth, the responsibility as well as the rights of humans—need to be proclaimed in such fashion.

In my work with the International Coordinating Committee on Religion and the Earth, I have taken the need for such a proclamation to heart. For the last two years I have worked with a unique process of interfaith consultations throughout the world to create an Earth Charter—a document that calls for commitment by people and nations to a set of principles that capture the spirit of the world that is now emerging.[9] I see the development of the Earth Charter as a useful consciousness-raising tool that involves many people in the process, and also provides a necessary focus for appropriate action. The Earth Charter, though still under development, served this purpose at the Earth Summit in 1992 as the nations of the world discussed the need for a statement of principles that recognized a new relationship between humanity and the Earth. Though such a charter was not adopted at that time, there is hope that the process will continue and that an Earth Charter will be signed by all nations at the fiftieth anniversary of the United Nations in 1995.

Conclusion

For human, Earth, and Spirit to (re)join in a mutually enriching relationship, the crisis we experience today needs to be understood at its most fundamental level: the alienation of humans from the Earth, that is born of fear, so that we do not feel that we belong, and that results in the creation of a world of illusory control to protect ourselves. The solution to our crisis, then, has to be the personal experience of the world as it truly is—a web of life—and our place in it. Only from such experience can a new understanding be reached that will allow us to take steps beyond our present tendency to patch things up and postpone changes that we must inevitably make.

When we experience the fire of the universe in the present moment, when our senses have been revitalized and our deep memory stirred, when we have been grasped by the mysterious purposes of the universe, then we will begin to know what to do, and, more importantly, have the power to do it. Our recovered sense of belonging will lead us to articulate new principles on which to build our lives and our institutions, and to foster their implementation through personal and organized community effort.

This, then, is the joining of human, Earth, and Spirit, long separated in lives and cultures, and now seeking reconciliation in a new era into which the human community and the natural world will enter, as a single sacred community, where we will learn again to dance to the rhythms of a common pulse.

✦ 5 ✦

The Soul and the World

by DAVID WHYTE

The one who most truly can be accounted brave is the one
who knows the meaning of what is sweet in life and what
is terrible, and then goes out undeterred to meet what is
to come.

—Pericles

It may be that the universe, being so profoundly interwoven
and harmoniously patterned, even in its chaotic aspects, wished
to discover itself in a new way and so created the one creature
which had the possibility of limping slightly out of step. Ourselves.
As human beings we look at the rain forest and see an ecology made
up of thousands of species that fit together exquisitely. Seeing this,
we intuit a life where we also have that possibility of fitting exquisitely. The prospect is both inspiring and redolent with grief. Seeing
that possibility draws us on even as it reinforces the bitterness of
our present exile from creation.

Our inability to come to terms with this exquisite fitting of the
world may be commensurate with our wish for immunity from its
terrors. We wish to experience nature's sublime beauty while keeping
its darker realities at arm's length. The Earth may be our mother but
it is also a turbulent partner that can be terrifying in its implacability.
Much of our distance from nature has come through a feeling of well-
earned rest after millennia of being at the mercy of many of its vagaries
and difficulties. In the throes of our industrial dreamtime, we are
waking astonished now, to find that our bid for immunity from the

58

storm cycles of existence comes at an equally *terrifying* cost—the integrity of the very life systems that support us.

At some time in our spiritual evolution there occurred a palace coup. The strategic part of the mind that had evolved to help each person and community survive to produce the next generation, became overconcerned for our *individual* safety. In some ways it put our possibilities for survival above our firsthand experience of existence itself. Brooding like an interior dictator, it finally took over the central territory of the psyche previously occupied by the soul. We became slaves to a form of individual safety that has never existed and that robbed us of our own intimate link with life itself. We withdrew from our own true home, the *Oikos,* the ecological home of our firsthand experience. From that point, safety through the holding of power over the otherness of the world, rather than the terrible and joyous experience of otherness itself, became the touchstone of human existence.

It may be that the most righteous ecological action we can take now is the cultivation of soul life, the life of texture, color, character, and firsthand experience; the meeting with life's astonishing otherness on a daily basis; a life worth living in the here and now; a life of firsthand desire that puts personal destiny as an equal partner with personal survival; the life that is sufficient through its own joining with the world it encounters; a life that does not need to use up everything it encounters in order to feel safe.

Our bid for safety is terribly hard on the world but easy on our selves, and yet our immunity from life's harder knocks remains a stubborn illusion. Human life itself may have a single whispered admonition at the center of its care-filled years. "There is no immunity . . ." Refusing that voice we will use up the whole world and its treasure rather than meet the soul's primary hunger for experience.

The soul's desires are easy on the world but hard on ourselves. The stakes are very high: we can live like refugees from a *Sharper Image* catalogue, surrounded by everything we think we need, seemingly immune, athletic and protected, while our feet slide beneath us, trying to find purchase as the ground support of life's primary and sacred otherness slips slowly away, or we can become human again, and limping slightly out of step, live on the solid ground of our own experience, joined to the unfathomable mystery of a vast and vital system.

* * *

The following poem, "Millennium," is my summation of everything we have to face at this point in history. Its central metaphor of fire I see as an abiding image for our time. What is marvelous about fire is its ability to hold two qualities simultaneously. First it is a source of tremendous nourishment: it warms hands, cooks food, and forms the center of our hearths and homes, the place where family or community gathers. But it is also the consuming elemental form; it carries the dance of energy that devours and sublimates the outworn. It seems to me that we cannot have one without the other and that this timeless human relationship with fire has much to teach us.

Millennium

The years pass quickly
but only frighten
by their speed in the backward view.

These times are times for holding on,
speaking out, stepping carefully
between the broken crystal of a culture

swept from a table filled with too much
for too few. There are no excuses
now and the places left to hide are visible to all.

The glass was broken because it was
broken from the beginning.
The journey begun because the body

takes a step in the first breath.
Wherever we go
we can only take a step from here,

and from wherever we came
we did not come from the place
where the mind waits in safety.

Before humans and as humans
we came from some kind of fire.
The supernova relived in the paint brush

touching cave walls and canvas.
Vision flaring in the hand-held light,
father to son, mother to child.

The fire in the earth first kindling
the flame, the hearth
where we gathered. The center of life

looking out into darkness
made sacred by light.

We needed that center then and shared
our food round that
warming pivot of explosive light.

Now darkness refuses the
periphery, seeping back
along the life lines we used as distance.

Back into the center of safety
where we drew
our sure indignant line of identity.

No one can be ashamed of fear.
Our inheritance is a sense of lack.

And small comfort now
our love of owning
will suddenly not suffice.

Our lives now center on experience
and the fire of its consuming.

Warmed and grown in its light
we prepare our metamorphosis in flame.

Easy the flame of the living death.
Easy the suicidal rush to arms
and the living death-wish of battle.

The way we have gone before.
The way we have rushed to oblivion.
The way we have bargained with life,

giving our life to the wrong life,
hoping many wrong lives consumed
would become as we ate, the one life of desire.

And standing still,
saying I, and the small vision I have
—is enough, becomes the hardest path of all.

The path where we have fallen
refusing to rise again
becomes the spiral line
of flame
where we turn
into the one desire
we have not lived.

The path opens before our eyes
turning into open country,
the wilderness
becomes the path of paths.

Now is the path
of leaving the path.

And we hear our own voice
demanding of ourselves
a faith in no-path,
when there is no faith at all.

And moving forward takes feral courage,
opens the wildest
and most outrageous light of all,

becomes the hardest path of all.
The firm line we drew in the sand
becomes the river we will not cross.

But the river of the soul flows on
and the soul
refuses safety until it finds the sea.

The ocean of longing,
the sea of your deepest want,
the gravity well of your own desire,

the place you would fall becomes
in falling
the place you are held.

The great sea
and the still ship of your own
becoming.

But still, on the ocean, there is
no path

only the needle's trembling dance
north

toward the new millennium, followed
without fear,

though the dance now is fear and calmness
in one movement

seeing

as you look
not only the angry sea
of what you
have denied

but
here,
near at hand,
in the center
of your body,

the rose-fire
of the compass
blossoming
with direction.[1]

✦ 6 ✦

Cosmogenesis

by BRIAN SWIMME

The universe flared forth fifteen billion years ago in a trillion-degree blaze of energy, constellated into a hundred billion galaxies, forged the elements deep in the cores of stars, fashioned its matter into living seas, sprouted into advanced organic beings, and spilled over into a form of consciousness that now ponders and shapes the evolutionary dynamics of Earth.

These are, as scientists like to say, the "facts." But what do we do with them? How does the fact of cosmogenesis—this great fact that is the culminating achievement of millions of humans laboring now for a hundred thousand years, developing technical languages, amassing empirical details, pursuing the ancient bewitching promise that we would come to know the mysteries of the universe—how does the discovery of cosmogenesis affect human consciousness?

I think those philosophers are correct who predict that over the next few centuries this knowledge will work its way deep into the strata of human consciousness, and will blossom into the fourth great mutation of Homo sapiens.

But I could be wrong. And many thoughtful people think I am. It's embarrassing for me now to admit that it took me many years to take their dismissals seriously. Awash in the study of cosmogenesis, energized by the astounding news of how the universe and life and human consciousness emerged, I was simply too fascinated with this story even to notice those who were not.

I do remember puzzling over Malcolm Muggeridge who announced one fine day that "no matter what scientists discover about the universe," nothing would change his fundamental worldview, which happened to be an evangelical form of Christianity. Apparently, (though at the time I was not capable of believing this) an intelligent person could remain unmoved by the empirical discovery of the universe's emergence into existence.

Another encounter that forced me to reflect took place when I was presenting some of the details of cosmogenesis at a conference in Santa Barbara. My single theme was that a new form of consciousness was emerging, one grounded in the story of cosmogenesis—the story of a universe beginning with the so-called Big Bang and unfolding through fifteen billion years to become this Great Community we find ourselves within. Soon after my presentation the psychologist James Hillman took the podium and announced: "I don't give a hill of beans about the Big Bang. In fact, I care more about beans than I do about the Big Bang!"

Nor could I conveniently chalk up such dismissals as resulting from the inadequate science education in the United States. My third and final example involves a preeminent physicist, Steven Weinberg, a Nobel laureate. Weinberg ends his book on the birth of the universe with this memorable line: "The more the universe seems comprehensible, the more it also seems pointless." Now this was truly baffling. Here was someone who knew everything I did about the birth of the universe and yet he concluded that such knowledge was without value, or that its only value was in the assistance it could provide us in reaching the conclusion that the universe was meaningless.

Why such a disparity of responses to this great fact?

Natural scientists such as myself are prone to examine anything but their own consciousness. This comes from a peculiar attitude common to our profession that is convinced the facts are what really matter. Not just that they are important. We have a deep faith that if we can just figure out what the facts of the matter are, we will be home free. Perhaps it was such confidence that enabled me to remain convinced, for two decades, that the empirical facts of cosmogenesis—all by themselves—were enough to launch our species into a new understanding. I never took seriously the notion that this great transformation of consciousness might involve something within, something having to do with experience.

The question that intrigues me now is this: "What is it that happens that leads a person to regard cosmogenesis not just as a scientific theory, or a string of empirical facts, but as a way of life, as a religious attitude that enables a fresh, and creative, and cosmological orientation within the world?"

I don't have the answer to this vast question, but I do have a story that might shed some light on it.

This took place on Halloween. I was wandering with my wife, Denise, and our two sons through the dark streets. Near the end of the night, worn-out, I decided to let the three of them go ahead and fleece the remaining houses on the cul-de-sac. To ease the pain in the small of my back, I crouched down close to the ground. There it happened. For just one moment, I left "California" and entered the "universe."

Because I do happen to live in California, a home of extraterrestrial abductions, endless spiritual channeling, and a hundred other highly imaginative and exotic experiments in consciousness, I need to state at once that I am speaking here of the most ordinary thing. I was just crouched down in the middle of the street. In one sense, nothing at all extraordinary took place. I was just crouched there.

It had been raining softly all evening. I was close to the ground and I noticed the thousand edges of black asphalt glittering with soft points of light from a street lamp overhead. For some reason all my roles seemed to vanish, or drop out of sight. I was no longer "Dad," or "husband," or "college teacher," or "Californian." I was not primarily in a "city." I was not part of a "holiday" of the "United States." I was suddenly just there, just this being, breathing, in the mist, rained upon, thinking.

Such tremendous things had to happen before I could crouch there. Vast galactic storms. Explosions so violent they were beyond the reaches of the human imagination. Subtleties of cellular electricity in a quintillion prokaryotes. I could not recount them all consciously, but I could feel them in a sense. I rode upon them as if I were treading water at midnight in the middle of an ocean with a deep current flooding up from below me. I sat crouched, amazed at the story that we now know, and amazed at the story of greatness that we would never know, that would stay hidden forever in the chasms of the past, but a story that had even so unfurled over billions of years into this moment, this experience, this present.

I was stupefied to reflect that this being that I was could have found itself in so many different forms. This breathing thing could be crouched in the bush of the great plains while its bonded mate gave birth to a new face off in the darkness. Could have huddled starving outside a cave that had been snowbound for thousands of years. This here-now could be inside the night of a peaceful Paleozoic swamp, or screaming with reptilian terror in an ancient tropical forest. And this crouched and breathing being was now surrounded by those same opaque mysteries that, for unfathomable reasons, had taken on the form of asphalt.

Something moved. Crawling into my moment was a narrow black insect. She too was suddenly just there. I didn't know her name, but she was drenched. She was moving very slowly. To me she seemed hesitant, or confused. She changed directions uselessly.

Crouched down, I met her on a primordial level. I found myself thinkng that she would never comprehend "asphalt," or "California," or "humanity." I sat staring, thinking how she was unable to read up on the situation. Unable to learn how to deal with roads, unable to learn how humanity had emerged and had flung up a thousand changes impossibly beyond her capacity for understanding. Here before me was a mentality of astonishing capabilities, one brought forth through a four-hundred-million-year creative adventure, but a mentality unable to grok the meaning of finding herself in this sea of "asphalt."

I had learned years before that through some supremely mysterious process the molten lava of Earth had, over four billion years, transformed itself into organic life; but in that moment, crouched in the rain, I experienced this understanding directly. It had been decades since I had first learned that the same genetic language informed humans and insects, but now I could feel how I and this insect had been woven out of those same intelligent patterns. It had been so long since I first learned that all the elements of our solar system had been created in a star, and then scattered by a supernova blast five billion years ago; but here in the night I experienced directly how I shared a common flesh with my confused and struggling kin.

Of course, I realize now how vulnerable to ridicule all this is. What fun a *New York Times* type could have with this scientist going soft over an insect's plight! But in the moment such thoughts were the furthest thing from my mind. In the moment, I felt that I had suddenly understood, once again, the inner meaning of all our scientific studies.

The discovery of cosmogenesis is the discovery of a way of entering a more profound relationship with our cousins of this great community. On occasion, in an entirely haphazard manner, I have found my way into a brief taste of this experience. Haphazard because these moments are not planned; haphazard because in each such experience it feels as if it were for the first time, so effectively do I erase the memories of these experiences.

I end these reflections with two questions. First, is it the case that cosmogenesis remains just a scientific theory for those who have never experienced directly its truth? And second, is it possible that when humans begin consciously to create educational forms trained on evoking an embodiment of cosmogenesis, they will be activating the next era in the evolution of the Earth?

+ 7 +

Imagination, Gaia, and the Sacredness of the Earth

by DAVID SPANGLER

When the sun rises on the morning of January 1, 2000, it will undoubtedly be a dawn like any other, just another day in the Earth's four and a half billion year history. Nowhere is it recorded in the stones of the Earth, the currents of the ocean, or the tempests of the winds that that dawn shall herald some special event. Yet for much of humanity, it will mark the beginning of a new millennium.

This passage into the twenty-first century is a social invention. It is an act of cultural imagination, and as such it provides a catalyst for other similar acts of imagination on which our collective prosperity and health—and even our survival—may rest. It is an invitation to reexamine, reevaluate, and where necessary, change attitudes and habits of culture that increasingly prove dysfunctional on the interconnected planet that we inhabit.

Foremost among these acts of revisioning is a reimagination of our relationship to the world. For nearly three centuries, Western culture has progressively imagined itself as distinct and separate from the natural order, while concomitantly imagining that order as simply a dead, material resource to be used (and used up) according to humanity's will (or more specifically, according to the will of those governments and corporations capable of managing such exploitation). There is now a very real question whether these

70

images can continue or whether they spell disaster for all of us unless changed.

I take the position that we must reimagine the world and ourselves within it in ways that recognize and emphasize the interconnectedness and interdependency that exist within the natural order, an order from which we are not separate. To fail to do so will be to condemn our descendants to lives of increasing misery and danger.

One key area for this reimagination is that of spirituality, theology, and ethics. Given the anthropocentrism of these disciplines in Western traditions, the challenge now is to find images for an ecotheology and a bioethics that extend our context of spirituality to include the nonhuman aspects of the world. We strive to develop a spirituality that embraces Earth as a whole. We seek to reimagine Earth, spirit, and ourselves in ways that synthesize these three into a new wholeness that is healing and empowering. We seek, in the words of Thomas Berry, a "new story," a new myth.

This is vital work, but it is important to remember that the objective of this quest is not simply new images with which to replace those that have grown old and outmoded. What we are after is to change behavior, to embody a new life, and to express a new spirit. Images and myths are powerful tools that can assist this process, but they can also turn in our hands and become obstructions. They can become new beliefs and dogmas that substitute one orthodoxy for another without liberating us into the life of the holistic spirit that is our true goal. So the craft of reimagining Earth and spirit is a delicate one.

To illustrate my point, I want to examine one particular image of the Earth and of our relationship to it that has developed in recent years. This is the image of the world as a living being, an image emerging from a scientific theory known as the Gaia hypothesis. In the decade or so since its appearance, it has become a powerful image that is being widely used or discussed in scientific, philosophical, ecological, and spiritual circles. In some ways the image of Gaia has become a symbol for the ecological and spiritual sensibility that we are trying to understand and cultivate. As such, this image can illustrate both the problems and pitfalls, and the advantages and strengths, involved in reimagining Earth and spirit.

In 1979, James Lovelock, a British atmospheric chemist and inventor, published a book called *Gaia: A New Look at Life on Earth.* In it he presented a theory called the Gaia hypothesis that he had developed in collaboration with American microbiologist, Lynn Margulis. This theory basically stated that the Earth's climate and surface environment are controlled by the planet's biosphere, in effect by all the microorganisms, plants, and animals that live upon and within the world. The core of the theory is that the planet functions as if it were a single living organism. At the suggestion of British novelist William Golding, a neighbor and friend of Lovelock, this planet-sized organism was named *Gaia* after the Greek goddess of the Earth.

Had Lovelock called his theory something more prosaic and scientific, like the Theory of Atmospheric and Environmental Regulation through Biospheric Homeostasis, our story would end here. The idea would have wound its way along a customary path of being published in scientific journals and discussed at scientific conferences. Chances are, though, it would not have emerged from the world of scientific jargon and procedure into public view, nor become a significant idea influencing public debate in political, environmental, philosophical, and religious circles. Cybernetic feedback loops are simply not images capable of firing the imagination and launching revolutions; it is difficult to picture impassioned citizens storming the ramparts of the status quo carrying banners proclaiming "Biospheric Homeostasis or Death!"

Gaia, on the other hand, is exactly such an image. It is the picture of an ancient goddess, arriving on the scene exactly as the feminine movement has been challenging the male, patriarchal view of the world. It resonates with very ancient cosmologies held in nearly every culture of the Earth at one time or another that recognized and affirmed the Earth as a living being possessed of soul. It therefore touches us at a deep level of racial memory and myth.

During a personal visit with James Lovelock in the early eighties, I asked him what the responses had been within the scientific community to his hypothesis. He said that there was interest, but that generally it had been ignored. (This has since changed. In 1988, the American Geophysical Union devoted its entire biannual conference to a discussion and evaluation of the Gaia hypothesis, and since then, the idea has become an accepted theoretical basis for further experimentation and study.) On the other hand, to his surprise, the idea had been taken up enthusiastically by religious and spiritual groups around the world, and that he received hundreds of lecture invitations from such groups. However, in an industrial culture challenged by ecological degradation as well as by a growing feminist sensibility, and therefore looking for new guiding myths, this response is not surprising at all. The idea of Gaia, the living Earth, reunites us with the mythic, feminist, ecological, and spiritual imagination of our ancestors in the currently acceptable form of a scientific image.

Gaia as a mythic idea is definitely alien to the original Gaia hypothesis as developed by James Lovelock and Lynn Margulis. Though it does conceive of the Earth as a living entity, such a being, in the words of Margulis, if conscious at all, has the sentiency "of an amoeba." Hardly the stuff of myth and spiritual invocation. But subjected to the forces of reimagination now going on in our culture, this hypothesis could hardly remain within the more sterile boundaries of "good" science. It is simply too fertile and too powerful an image. So it has exploded to become a one-word hieroglyph suggesting an organizing principle—the central paradigm—of an entire new cultural outlook. In fact, as suggested by such book titles as *Gaia: A New Way of Knowing,* a compilation of essays edited by cultural historian, William Irwin Thompson, Gaia has come to signify a whole epistemology based on a holistic or systems view of the world.

Gaia has also taken on spiritual implications. After all, it was originally the name of a goddess. While in its modern usage it is generally not used to refer to or reinvoke that ancient Grecian deity, it is often used to suggest the existence of a world soul or spirit. I have attended Christian worship services where in a spirit of progressiveness and ecological correctness, the participants call upon the "spirit of Gaia" to heighten their awareness of their connections with the Earth. In such a context, Gaia is not used to refer to deity but, rather, to a kind of oversoul or purposeful planetary spiritual presence, like an archangel presiding over the well-being and wholeness of the world, or perhaps in a more psychological sense, as a collective awareness arising from all the lives, human and nonhuman, that make up our Earth.

So Gaia is used as an image to reimagine the nature of the Earth and of our relationship to it; it is also being used to reimagine the spiritual nature of our planet, since if it is a living being and possesses a soul or spirit of some kind, then we cannot view it simply as "dead matter." If there is a relationship God has to us as living beings, then that relationship also extends to and includes the Earth. If we may participate in sacredness, then so does the Earth, not simply as a valued and cherished environment but as a fellow creature. Furthermore, by virtue of being a *world,* a context that embraces and nourishes trillions of other lives and provides for their embodiment, the spiritual presence of the Earth may have qualities and capabilities exceeding our own. Again, it might be seen as a kind of archangel or guiding spirit implementing and fulfilling God's plan for the Earth.

However we view it, the image of Gaia as a living being is a powerful one filled with unexplored implications for reimagining ourselves, Earth, and spirit. What, though, are some of the pitfalls and potentials involved in using this particular image in this way?

I have already mentioned that the idea of a living Earth and of a world soul is an ancient one, one found in nearly every culture that has existed on Earth except (until now) our own. Gaia reinvokes this sensibility in our modern, materialistic, industrial culture. However, a reinvocation is not the same as a reincarnation. The sense of a living Earth enjoyed and practiced by earlier, nonindustrial cultures grew out of living experience and a closeness to nature that our culture has set aside. It was interwoven into the fabric of life and culture, and it was often part of a matriarchal perspective, or at least one that honored the feminine side of divinity. This is not true for us.

Furthermore, the Judeo-Christian tradition arises from the Semitic spiritual perspective of God and creation being separate and distinct, as well as from patriarchal social structures. In such a context, sacredness has overtones of authority, power, distance, and maleness that would have been alien to the spirituality of, for instance, the ancient Celts or the Native Americans, two cultures that incorporated a sense of the living Earth. This means that when we strive to imagine the sacredness of the Earth, we do so in a very different cultural context than did those who took for granted an immanent, accessible, sacred presence pervading all things.

Can we simply adopt and graft onto our culture their notion of a living, sacred Earth? I don't think so, at least not without distortion. We have to think deeply into and live out this idea in a modern context. Until we do, Gaia, the spirit of the living Earth, is an idea to think about rather than an idea to think with. It is a novelty rather than a tacit assumption, and as a spiritual idea it can be superficial. It lacks the overtones and undertones—the deeper connections with our everyday life and with the mysteries of creation—that it possessed in earlier cultures. As an idea, it becomes a suit to try on, rather than a body to inhabit and live through.

When we talk about the spirit of Gaia, the spirit of a living Earth, or even of the Earth as being alive, just what do we mean in our time? Do we even have the same sense of life—of what being an entity means—as did our ancestors? We are the products of a materialistic, technological, rational, male-oriented culture that over two hundred years ago set aside the medieval notions of the Great Chain of Being in which each and every life had a purpose, a place, and a meaning. The importance of the bottom line has made us forget that there is a "top line" as well that gives the spiritual value—the holistic value—of a person, a plant, an animal, or a place. If at worst the bottom line represents how entities can be exploited and used for profit, the top line represents how entitites can both empower and be empowered for the good of the whole.

It is this sense of the whole and of the individual as an expression of the whole that we do not have. We have a sense of incarnation but not of coincarnation, of the many ways in which the fabric of our identities are interwoven and interdependent in ways extending far beyond just the human milieu. Thus our definitions of life become very reductionist, individualized, and utilitarian. What, then, does it mean to us to speak of the Earth as a living being, not in a biological sense but in a metaphysical sense?

Accepting Gaia simply as a "return of the Goddess" or jumping on the bandwagon of a new planetary animism without thinking through the implications of just what Gaia might mean in our culture can lead to sentimentality rather than spirituality. We think we have made a spiritual breakthrough when in fact we are simply indulging in a kind of romantic fantasy that lacks the power truly to reorganize our lives and our society. To invoke the "spirit of Gaia" is no substitute for hard-edged, practical political, economic, and scientific work to redress the ecological imbalances currently endangering us. If the idea of Gaia is to inform, empower, and sustain our culture to make the hard choices and difficult changes necessary to secure our children's future, then it must be more than just a clever, sweet, or sentimental image.

I believe Gaia is an important spiritual idea for our time, but for it to fulfill its potential, we must remember that a spiritual idea is not something we think about but something that inhabits and shapes us. It is like a strand of DNA, organizing and energizing our lives. A spiritual idea is not just another bit of data to be filed away. It is incarnational rather than descriptive, coming alive only when incorporated (made flesh) in our lives through work, practice, effort, skill, and reflection. It becomes part of the foundation and the architecture of our lives. Being a new icon for worship is not enough. Invoking the spirit of Gaia is insufficient unless we understand just how we shape and participate in that spirit and in turn are shaped by it.

However, a deeper question is do we really need Gaia as a spiritual image? Do we need another spiritual source, another presence to invoke? If there is a true Spirit of the Earth, a Planetary Logos, is it hierarchically superior to humanity? That is, does it stand somewhere between ourselves and God? If so, we run the risk of interposing yet another image between ourselves and divinity. Or if the Earth is seen as sacred, just what does that mean? Why should the Earth be conceived of as sacred simply because it is alive? Do we extend the same privilege to other living things? Is life alone the criterion for sacredness? Or does something become sacred when it is living and powerful, big and capable of doing us either harm or good? Does Gaia become a substitute for God? What would such a substitution mean? Does it bring God closer to us, or does it further muddy the meaning and nature of God, making it yet more difficult to determine clearly just what the sacred is and what our relationship is to it?

These are important questions. There *is* a strong desire to affirm the sacredness of all life and of the Earth as a whole. However, the object of this exercise, it seems to me, is not to come up with new images of divinity but to affect behavior. What we really want is to relate to ourselves, to each other, and to the world as a whole as if we all have ultimate value apart from utilitarian considerations. If something is sacred, it is assumed to have value beyond its form, its usefulness, its duration, and its products. It is valuable and precious in and for itself. It is worthy of respect and honor, love and compassion; it is worth entering into communion with it. Its very being is its only justification; it needs no other.

As things stand, before we can manipulate or exploit something or someone, we must first devalue them, making them lower than ourselves. That which is sacred cannot be devalued, and by naming the Earth and all upon it as sacred, we seek to protect it and ourselves from ourselves. Perhaps, though, this is a form of psychological overkill. Can we not value something just for itself without needing to assign it a special place or condition in the universe? Can we not behave with love and respect for the environment for reasons other than that we come to consider it sacred? The implication is that we would then consider anything that is simply ordinary and not sacred to be fair game for whatever rapacious and manipulative desires we may choose to act upon—which, when you think about it, is a fair description of precisely how much of humanity does act.

By using the image of Gaia to give the Earth special status, we do not really deal with the question of our unwise and uncaring behavior. We are simply setting up a boundary within which we will be good, much as someone will act nicely on Sundays in church and act in a mean-spirited way the rest of the week. Surely, we are being called to a deeper reevaluation and reimagination of human behavior, one that transforms our attitudes and behavior toward each other and the world not because of a label but because it is right to do so.

Turning Gaia into a mythic or spiritual idea may be inappropriate or premature, leading both to misplaced concreteness and misplaced spirituality. On the other hand, Gaia can be an *inspirational* idea. Such an idea, to me, is like an enzyme. It is not important in itself except as it catalyzes a process. An enzyme is a means toward something else, a component of a larger emergence. In this context,

Gaia would be an enzyme of consciousness, promoting and aiding a process of expanding our awareness in at least six areas important to our time.

The first of these is the most obvious. The idea of Gaia heightens our awareness of ecological and environmental necessities and responsibilities. It inspires us to translate theory and concern into practical strategies to preserve the environment and to meet ecological crises.

The second area of awareness follows on from this. Gaia shifts our operating paradigm from a mechanical one based on classical physics to an ecological one based on biology. It puts the phenomenon of life itself back into center stage in our culture. It inspires us toward a reformation that produces a culture that is truly life affirming and life centered.

Third, because the phenomenon of life as expressed through organisms and ecologies of organisms manifests more than the sum of its parts, it cannot be understood using solely analytical and reductionist techniques or modes of thought. Thus, Gaia represents an epistemology as well, a way of learning, seeing, and knowing. It inspires us to develop modes of thinking and acting that are holistic, systemic, symbiotic, connective, and participatory. We must learn to see the world in terms of patterns and not just positions and points, in terms of networks and lattices, not just centers and peripheries, in terms of processes, not just objects and things. We are encouraged to develop and practice an "ecology of mindfulness," to paraphrase anthropologist Gregory Bateson, as well as a mindful ecological practice. It inspires us to act toward each other as well as toward the environment in ways that serve and nourish the whole of which we are all participants, and in ways that are compassionate and cocreative, cooperative, and coincarnational.

Fourth, the image of Gaia *does* inspire us to think of the spirituality of the Earth and to explore an "eco-theology." Such a spirituality is important, for beyond ecology and conservation lies a deeper dimension of spiritual interaction and communion with our environment that is mutually important for ourselves and for nature. Within that dimension as well we will find new insights into the meaning of the divine that cannot help but aid us in the emergence of a healthy and whole planetary culture.

Fifth, religion is always defining the sacred in a way that creates boundaries, including some things and excluding others, and then finds itself trapped by its very boundaries. God must laugh at this, but for human beings it can have tragic circumstances, as witness the innumerable religious wars throughout history. A fundamentalist Christian once informed me with frightening sincerity that the only people who had souls, and thus could be considered human beings, were people who had been born again through believing in Jesus Christ. All other people were not human at all but soulless animals who, like all animals and plants and physical matter in general, lay outside God's love and concern and were destined for destruction anyway. So it did not matter what happened to them or what one did to them. They were here simply to be used by true Christians until the coming of the millennium.

Of course, this is an extreme and profoundly non-Christian and unbiblical view that should be rejected by any follower of the Nazarene. However, it is removed only in degree from the more mainstream Christian viewpoint that only humans have souls and that the nonhuman world is therefore of little spiritual consequence and can be used as we wish. In either case, the idea of the sacred is being used as a boundary to exclude some part of creation from having any ultimate value. By calling the Jews nonhuman, the Nazis justified the Holocaust. By regarding the nonhuman, natural world as outside the sacred community defined by a particular religious viewpoint, and therefore outside of moral consideration and subject only to the kind of utilitarian and economic judgments we reserve for objects, we are engaging in another kind of Holocaust. It is the natural world we are feeding into the ovens of overconsumption and technological arrogance. Only this time, because of the interrelatedness of the biosphere, we are all of us—human and nonhuman—becoming the new Jews, heading toward what philosopher and environmentalist Roger Gottlieb calls "Auschwitz Planet."

By expanding our boundaries of the sacred to include all the nonhuman cosmos, we give ourselves a much larger definition of God, a greater community of life in which to dwell, and a larger definition of ourselves as well, since part of how we define ourselves is influenced by how we define the sacred and our relationship to it. Given the comparative size of the human world to the immensity, diversity, and richness of the nonhuman cosmos, it is only the greatest of arrogance that seizes for ourselves the central role in a creation drama, relegating the rest of the universe to playing a supporting role or, at worst, being simply a backdrop for our struggles and adventures. Learning to see the sacredness of the Earth and the cosmos beyond may reintroduce into our culture some needed perspective and some creative humility, a word that itself comes from the same root word as *humus,* meaning "of the soil."

Finally, Gaia provides a mirror in which to see ourselves anew. It inspires us to reflect on our own natures, on the meaning and destiny of humanity. Lovelock paved the way for this in his book *Gaia.* In the last chapter, he suggested that humanity might be the evolving nervous system of the Earth, the means by which Gaia achieves self-awareness. At a time when our society seems motivated by no higher purpose than endless expansion and the making of money, and when humanity seems to have no purpose beyond itself, this image is striking and refreshing. It would seem to suggest a direction, a connection, a role that we can play in a world that is more than just the sum total of human desires.

This image of humanity as nervous system can be a helpful, guiding metaphor if we define the nervous system in a systemic and dynamic way. If by nervous system we mean the wiring that carries the sensations and thoughts of a larger being, then that is not a particularly participatory image, for it reduces humanity to being simply the instrumentality for the transmission and execution of the thoughts of the Earth.

However, if by nervous system we mean the whole system that governs, guides, and controls the organism through reception and integration of sensation and the transmission of thought, then such a nervous system is more than just wiring. As modern medicine and biochemistry increasingly show, the whole body is an integrated sensing and directing organism. Glands, hormones, blood, circulation, physical structure, and interrelationships between organs play as much a role in structuring and transmitting "thought" as does the nervous system itself. Thus, to be the "nervous system" of the Earth really means to be integrated with all the systems of the Earth, from wind and weather to tidal flows and the growth of plants, from the ecology of watersheds to the migration of birds and insects from one bioregion to another, and so on. It means *being* Gaia in a way that transcends and enlarges our humanity. Just what that really involves is what we have to discover, but surely it goes beyond accepting without reflection pat slogans about Gaia and the sacredness of the Earth.

The image of Gaia enlarges our vision of human purpose and activity beyond the personal and the local and puts it into a planetary and cosmic context. At the same time, the actions of Gaia are very local and specific, so that we are made more aware, not less, of our interactions with the particular places we inhabit. This is an important shift in our time.

Gaia *is* an important idea, both as a scientific hypothesis and as a spiritual image. I see it as a transitional idea. It is not so much a revelation in itself as a precursor to revelation or to new insights that can come when that idea is examined and lived with and given a chance to settle into our bones. Its meaning now lies in what it can inspire us to discover about ourselves and the nature of life, in rallying our energies to meet the needs of our environment, and through these processes of discovery and healing, to become a truly planetary species.

Gaia is not the only image we could use to reimagine our relationship to the Earth or to develop a new understanding of the spirituality of the Earth. Yet, however we perform this reimagination and whatever images we may come up with to guide us into the future, for an image truly to live for us so that it weaves into our everyday lives and guides our daily behavior, it cannot be simply imported or remembered. It cannot be grafted on from the outside or from the past. It must emerge from our own personal and cultural experiences of pain and joy in connection with the larger planetary environment. It must emerge from our own contemporary act of embodied imagination. It must emerge as our own act of collective learning that creates a new bond of community between ourselves and the natural order.

We cannot simply take up the mind-sets of our ancestors nor wear their myths as if we have not changed in the interim between their world and time and ours. We cannot *assume* the sacredness nor spiritual livingness of the Earth or accept it as a new ideology or as a sentimentally pleasing idea. We must experience that life and sacredness, if it is there, in relationship to our own and to that ultimate mystery we call God. We must experience it in our lives, in our practice, in the flesh of our cultural creativity. We must allow it to shape us, as great spiritual ideas have always shaped those who invite them in. We must not expect that we can simply use these new images, such as the image of Gaia, to meet emotional, religious, political, or even commercial needs without allowing them to transform us in unexpected and radical ways. The spirituality of the Earth is more than a slogan. It is an invitation to initiation, to the death of what we have been and the birth of something new.

✦ 8 ✦

Earth Is Our Home
by SUSAN OSBORN

I have been a singer nearly all of my life and song is woven through my identity and my deepest friendships and loves. For me, there is nothing superficial about this great out-pouring that moves through me. This primal creative act has instructed me in the basics—that singing is a physical metaphor and experience of the act of creation, that singing together is an act of honoring differences and creating communion, and that song is in essence an integrative act. It has always been difficult for me to define myself as either a performer or an entertainer. Rather, as I grew with song, I began to see myself as a kind of musical diplomat sharing the universal language of music.

In June of 1991, I was asked by a Japanese record producer, Masato Ushijima, to help create and sing an album of traditional and familiar Japanese melodies in English with jazz and pop arrangements. He told me that he wanted to give these beautiful songs back to the Japanese people in a new form, with the hope that they would remind them of their culture's basic and profound love and connection with nature, expressed in the Japanese word *Wabi*. This was to become the album's title. As we worked on this album, we began to feel that these songs could create a bridge from Japan to the rest of the world.

One of my first tasks was to help create English lyrics for these simple and subtle songs. The traditional song, "Furusato," is about the love of one's hometown, the people, and the land. On a train to Hotaka from Tokyo, I wrote new lyrics that are a translation of the feeling about home expressed in the original "Furusato." This song was chosen for use in a film about the Voyager spacecraft project being made for television by the brilliant Japanese filmmaker, Jin Tatsumura. It is played with the images of Earth taken from Voyager. This new version of "Furusato" is intended to express a feeling of love and connection to Earth, as our home, and along with the original universal melody, to create an Earth anthem. Here are the words to "Earth Is Our Home":

> Forests of green and gold
> Prairies so wide
> Wild rushing rivers, mountains so high
> Crystal skies and fields of grain
> Miracles of sun and rain
> Beauty surrounds me
> Earth is my home
>
> Deep running salmon
> Slumbering bear
> Geese flying north again, red colt and mare
> Leaping deer and sounding whale
> Winging dove and crawling snail
> Family of living things
> Earth is my home
>
> Memories of childhood, timeless and true
> Memories of family, memories of you
> Laughter and lonely tears
> Brightest hopes and darkest fears
> We share this humanity
> Earth is our home

Reimagining the
Role of the Human
in the Earth Community

by SHARON DALOZ PARKS

I have begun to recognize that I am fascinated and sometimes dismayed by how we do or don't change our minds, grow into emotional maturity, discover truth, and are healed. I am in awe of our capacity to be transformed and our resistance to it. My attention is drawn again and again to the wonder and terror of our participation in this drama of knowing and not knowing, and the strengths and limits of our capacity to see and to understand. I have become a teacher, a researcher, a counselor, and a professor, continually intrigued with the courage and costs of human becoming and increasingly deeply moved, warmed, sobered, or anguished by a sense of all that is at stake in whether or not we apprehend as faithfully as possible the nature of self and world.[1]

Three decades ago, the effort to understand this kind of faithfulness took me first, not so much into "educational theory" (as important as that is), but rather into a more primary contemplation. I began to see the significance of understanding the process of imagination.[2] But it is only in much more immediate time that I am coming to see how vital it is that we bring an understanding of the imagination to the spiritual challenge at the heart of the environmental crisis. At the core of this spiritual challenge lies the task of reimagining the role of the human within the small planet home we share—within a universe of mystery and disclosure.

Who are we human beings? Why are we here? What are we doing? What is our power? What are the limits of our power? Is the Earth ours to use? To use up? To steward? To depend upon? Why do we know how to make and use tools? Why do we have the power to reflect upon our action? Why do we have the power to take the perspective of another? Is the Earth asking something of us? Does the Earth need us? Are we interdependently woven into a powerful pattern of ongoing creation with a fitting part to play—a part we have not yet adequately apprehended? Is there something that is trying to get our attention? Are we being called?

When considered most profoundly, these questions of role and purpose are questions of vocation. Frederick Beuchner has elegantly and rightly recognized that vocation is the place where the heart's deep gladness meets the world's deep hunger.[3] We have been asked to live in a time that requires us to reconsider what it is that nourishes the heart's deep gladness and to recognize more adequately the character of the world's deep hunger—the nature, purposes and possibilities of life itself.

Accordingly we are being invited, even tugged, toward the formation of a new imagination. Imagination must not be confused with fantasy. A fantasy may delight or terrorize, but it is not "reality." In contrast, the disciplined imagination, as Samuel Taylor Coleridge recognized it, is the highest power of the knowing mind. It is the faculty by which we may grasp what is real, true, and trustworthy. Imagination is the sturdy and vulnerable process by which we compose and are composed. Imagination is the process by which we grasp (or fail to grasp) reality and thereby make meaning of self and world. We live and die according to what we see/imagine—and fail to see/imagine—as real and meaningful.

Our imaginations are now being called to the tasks of a challenging age. We live in a time of pervasive paradigmatic shift. What is going on at the deepest levels of personal and social life is a struggle for a meaningful, viable image of the future. A very fine bishop who is even more of a poet, Robert Morneau, has observed that there are now two images that dominate the human imagination: the mushroom cloud and the Earthrise—the image of the Earth as seen from space. These images are new images. Neither of these images were planted in the human imagination fifty years ago. One of these images evokes fear. The other evokes hope. We live in a time of unprecedented fears and unprecedented challenges and possibilities.

The mushroom cloud is a "triumph" of our scientific and political imagination as it has taken form since the nineteenth century. This image also serves as a metaphor for an ethic of control, an ethic centered in the illusion of individual and national dominance. The image of Earth as seen from space—also a "triumph" of the scientific and political imagination—compels us to recognize a necessary ethic of interdependence, responsibility, vulnerability, and risk.[4]

The imagination of domination and its illusion of control is tenacious. The imagination of petrochemical, industrial/technological consumerism has developed very sophisticated modes of maintaining itself. Driven in significant measure by the increasing power of market logic, contemporary marketing expertise is employed to work its way with the human imagination (as a master rather than a tool), if we will let it. Our mere cynicism about TV advertisements is but one indicator of our illusion of control. We may be cynical and "aware," but we do not remain unaffected. Indeed, images and their accompanying values and yearnings are daily and relentlessly being planted at the heart's core through modern media. More, they are being orchestrated, meaning that those who have reflected on the nature of the human imagination so as to place it in the servitude of market logic have taken pains to understand the imagination, not only as images, but as a complex process. For good and ill, such understanding makes attempts to craft and engineer the public soul possible. Our patterns of desire—our "choices" of dress, play, food, travel, work, entertainment, politics, and even friendship are increasingly the creation of someone else's understanding of our imagination.

If we are going to reimagine the role of the human in the service of more meaningful, fitting, and faithful living in relationship to the natural environment upon which our very lives depend, we cannot defer to others such understanding. We too must understand the process by which the human imagination participates in the weaving of our common life. What is the nature of this process?

Briefly, the broad contours of the process of imagination may be described as a series of five movements:[5]

1. *Conscious Conflict:* The faithful imagination is prompted and nourished by conscious attention to dissonance, disjuncture, contradiction, ill fittingness, and confusion. The poet awakens us by placing the familiar with the unusual, the predictable with the unpredictable. If we are going to reimagine the role of the human, we will begin to attend to the juxtapositions that awaken us to reality—even though our first experience may be unfamiliar and dissonant. For example:

> The trees are our lungs.

Coming to terms with dissonance and contradictions that simultaneously seem important and/or intriguing may lead us yet further into disquieting information.

> "Wherever rain forests are found, they are under siege. . . . They are disappearing from the face of the Earth at the rate of one and a half acres a second, night and day, every day, all year round."[6] US taxpayers are subsidizing the paper industry's use of virgin timber as purchasers and disposers and as managers of the forest system, contributing to the reluctance to use recycled materials.[7]

Such information enhances our consciousness of the dissonances and awakens us to the consequences of our previously unreflected "choices." Our first experience of this consciousness may be a sense of complexity and conflict that not only informs but overwhelms. Thus the first movement in the process of reimagining the role of the human is this kind of coming to a sense of conscious conflict that awakens us—in this case to discomfort, but sometimes to delight. In either case, a motion prompted by an exquisite mix of dis-ease and attraction begins to form in the mind-soul and seeks resolution and completion.

2. *Pause:* When some conflict, dissonance, or not-yet-understood delight has become conscious, if it is going to serve our ongoing

becoming, it must be given the respect of our waiting. This is the movement (which may require seconds or years) when the mind is relaxed, but the soul keeps watch.[8] Here we do not escape from the conflict, but rather we give it our "relaxed attention." We sleep on it; we put it on the back burner; we meditate; we stop. We make time for the master currents of the soul to do their work at deep levels of our being—which are not given entirely into our keeping.

This need for pause that is set at the core of the well-functioning human organism reveals the toxicity of the busyness of our age. Busyness numbs and blocks this deep work of the faithful imagination, insuring that we will neither have to face the deep distress of the conflicts that beset us, nor will we be transformed. In contrast, if we do allow a space, a pause, we will be gifted with new images— new ways of more adequately apprehending and naming what is real and trustworthy.

3. *Image or Insight:* An image is an object or act of the sensible world that lends its form to simplify and unify what was previously disparate and dissonant. For example, as a culture, we have seen the human as over-against nature, other than nature, dominating nature, stewarding nature, controlling nature, at the mercy of nature. In each of these imaginations the human is separate from nature. Yet Joanna Macy has offered us a gift of her imagination:[9]

Eco-self.

The image of "eco-self" elegantly holds together—simplifies and unifies—the conflicted dichotomy of self and nature, the human and the Earth. As with all fitting images, a part of the power of this image is its "resonance." It connects with what is deep and habitual within us. Our long-established familiarity with the sound and concept "ego-self" along with our emerging respect for our ecosystem, prepares us to receive the image, "eco-self." This new image resolves the tension of the false separation between the human and the ecosystem, while simultaneously it moves us beyond the psychology and ethics of egocentric individualism into a more connected conviction. The new image, eco-self, begins to serve as a solvent, rendering more permeable our ethic of domination and control. We are awakened and moved into the opportunity to dwell in a new imagination.

4. *Repatterning:* Often the process of imagination stops with an image that only momentarily awakens and satisfies. We feel the "ah, ha!" of insight, yet life as it scurries on is not transformed. This is because the process of imagination is yet incomplete and because the next and fourth movement in the process requires an act of will. (While the image—the third movement—is always experienced as a gift, the other four movements require at least some degree of a more disciplined consciousness.) Here we must consciously make the connections between the image-insight and the rest of our knowing in order to recompose our daily reality in light of the new image. Failure to do so maintains the power of the former, deeply patterned "reality." Thus, we must exercise the care not only to receive the image but to contemplate it. In this case we do so by posing a question such as, "If we are eco-selves rather than merely ego-selves, what does that mean?" Perhaps it means that we can no longer speak of whether we will cherish loggers *or* old-growth forests—jobs *or* owls. We are invited to think more profoundly.

> Connect, for example, the intimate relationship between loggers as human beings with lungs, who like the rest of us, are dependent upon trees not only for livelihood but also for oxygen, and the fact that when the remaining ten percent of the Northwest old-growth forests are cut down, the loggers will still lose their jobs. Then add the awareness that the bark of the yew tree yields a cancer-fighting drug, and it takes the bark from four trees to treat one patient. Then add also that scientists are learning how to extract the same drug from the needles of the tree.

If we stay with this repatterning, connective activity, steadily making one connection after another (sometimes rapidly and sometimes painstakingly), we will come to recognize that we cannot choose between our economy and our ecology. Indeed, both words are rooted in *oikos* meaning household, and both ecology and economy touch essential features of human well-being.[10] Such repatterning of awareness begins to anchor new images and concepts in the fabric of our lives. We begin to become yet more at home in a new imagination, a new way of making meaning of self with world.

5. *Interpretation or Testimony:* This movement most profoundly reveals our interdependence with others in the human community. We humans are social creatures, and it seems that we are not fully anchored in a new knowing until we can express it for ourselves to one another. Our new knowing isn't complete within us until we have been able to say it out loud, or dance it, or write it, paint it, or live it—to act in a new way—and to receive confirmation from an invested public.

More, however, we need each other in this fifth movement in the imagination process because sometimes we grasp a seemingly brilliant but actually ill-fitting image. Here lurks the primary vulnerability of the human imagination—the possibility that we may grasp and cling to an inadequate image and the possibility that we will not have the community available to confirm or constructively contradict our images appropriately. We are saved from the limits of our own subjectivity only through community.

The faithful imagination is dependent upon communities of confirmation and/or constructive contradiction. For example, I was speaking recently with a woman who has markedly exercised a faithful imagination across many years. I discovered that for over a decade, she and her husband have been meeting twice a month with a small group who consciously choose to serve each other as a community of confirmation and constructive contradiction as they seek to cultivate and practice a faithful imagination. With reference to the importance of this group, she remarked in practical terms,

You know, you have to reorganize your kitchen.

When I looked puzzled, she elaborated, "If you are going to care about the environment, for example, and recycle paper and all the rest, you have to reorganize your kitchen, and it's harder to get around to doing that if you don't have a community of support and accountability."

We need this sort of community in immediate, interpersonal terms. Likewise, on behalf of our common, public life we also must create institutions of support and accountability that nourish an imagination of the common good. We need the neighborhood, the corporation, the state, and the nation to function as communities of confirmation and constructive contradiction. We need communities of public discourse that give form to practices, policies, and penalties that enable us to act on behalf of a new imagination embodied in new, more faithful modes of action. We—the public—need

> curbside recycling, industrial recycling, the development of alternative modes of livelihood for loggers, and a reexamination of tax and forest management practices.

But even this is not enough. The challenges before us now require us to enlarge yet further the scope of our community of confirmation and contradiction to include, not only the neighborhood, the corporation, the state, and the nation, but also the whole Earth community. For example, recognition of the significance of rain forests thousands of miles away, may foster

> a reordering of our dinner menus and reconsideration of international monetary policies and practices.

To bring our images and insights to the test of only "those like us" in merely class-bound and national terms, is to court an impoverished and finally dangerous imagination of the role of the human.

If we bring our "triumphs of imagination" to be tested in the context of both the whole human family (including those beyond the margins of the consumer societies) and our ecosystem, which together constitute our full household, we will surely court ongoing, seemingly endless conscious conflict. But just as surely we will discover that the role—the vocation—of the human is, in part, to be about the good and hard work of learning to receive and to cultivate an imagination by which the whole Earth community may dream and thrive.

Indeed, as Coleridge saw, the imagination is the power within us that can become one with Spirit—the power that "moved over the water at the dawn of Creation." It appears that we are distinct among the species in the combined power of our capacity for both reflection and for tool making. We are fascinated by our tools and what they can do in the service of our ethic of control. We have increasingly allowed this fascination with tools, with technology, to drive our choices by means of market logic, narrowly understood. Our imaginations have become harnessed and numb. The images of the mushroom cloud and the Earthrise can in their juxtaposition awaken us and invite us to recover the prior vocation of the imagination itself. We are invited to the good and hard work of disciplining the energies of the imagination by courageously facing dissonance and conflict, allowing and cultivating pause and reflection, nurturing worthy images, attending to repatterning, and practicing the arts of confirmation and constructive contradiction. If we say yes to the invitation, we will create and dwell in the place where the heart's deep gladness meets the world's deep hunger.

✦ *10* ✦

Reminded by Beauty

by BARRY HEREM

As an artist I believe in beautiful objects. They not only compel us and attract our attention, they even make us feel illuminated. It's true as well with music or with aspects of nature. There is something in great classical music that seems inevitable. It suggests the infinite. For example, in listening to Mozart, the life-giving feelings we have of pleasure and satisfaction come from the beauty, the perfect balance, and harmony of the music. There is a poignancy, something that strikes deeply in beautiful music, or in a beautiful object, great architecture, nature—in many things.

Of course the word *beauty* is subject to very many interpretations, but I think, personally, that one of the surest ways to gauge what is beautiful (if someone really needs to gauge it—after all, it is indefinable) is to ask, or observe, what ordinary people think. Ordinary people often have a way of responding to things just as they are, because of what they honestly look or feel like.

For me, the real essence of beauty is expressed in a haiku.

> Beauty recalls a
> former estate when
> we knew perfect harmony.

I think that beauty, however we see it or call it—whether in our children, in the shape of a musical phrase, or in nature—is like a bell that rings deeply in the back of the skull, and deep in the heart. It reminds us of another realm from which we have come, which was the embodiment of perfect harmony, a truly spiritual environment. I think that beauty always reminds us of that former estate that we have come from and forgotten. It's a totally religious, spiritual feeling about life. This consciousness doesn't start here, but our life is merely a continuance of a former existence that was ultimate beauty in spirit.

I am always in pursuit of this thing I call beauty. (Who wouldn't be with this kind of a belief system?) I pursue it in my own work, in the world, and in the people I make friends with. In people I think that beauty comes primarily from character, heroism, honesty, high-mindedness, and quite a lot of the humor that always puts a lovely, accessible ring around things. These sorts of lofty expressions don't really need defining, we know them when we see them and they make people beautiful. They are both ideals and ideas and maybe, ultimately, it's ideas that are the most beautiful things of all.

Beauty is innately political because the world is endlessly improved by beautiful thoughts, beautiful music, and beautiful objects. I think that when you are in a state of harmony, the kind of harmony that is evoked and recollected by whatever you find beautiful, then politics falls into place.

Anthony Burgess said something very interesting: "We are involved in a mystery which is the satisfaction of form." I don't know how beauty harmonizes one at all, or how form satisfies. How can you be in distress and listen to music that you love, that you find beautiful, and be soothed? How can you be soothed by an idea? Or any of these things? That's where the mystery is. And the mystery comes from some place we don't know much about. But I do believe that if you go about your business fearlessly, enjoying and furthering the cause of beautiful things, harmonious attitudes, compassionate ways, that then politics, and the social problems it represents, tend to evaporate. Certainly, as an embittering preoccupation, they do. A lot of difficulties simply change, vanish, when you reach out past them with the wish to see things differently.

The idea of beauty is a very potent force in the world, and it operates despite all the vicissitudes of style, and all the most fashionable ideas about it. It cannot be repudiated. It spiritualizes our experience of the world. Earth is dross without spirit and I think that the trail to degradation is forgetfulness. Nevertheless, the Earth remains a manifestation of spirit. We only need to remember. The function of beauty is to remind.

◆ *11* ◆

The View from the Grounds

by KURT HOELTING

On a clear day from the Fairweather grounds, off the outer coast of Glacier Bay National Park, I can see an astonishing geophysical display. A hundred and twenty miles to the north looms Mt. St. Elias. At eighteen thousand feet, it is an impressive peak, even at this distance. The St. Elias range drops off into Yakutat Bay and the ecologically rich Yakutat Forelands, hidden on the northeastern horizon. Then the Earth rears back up, revealing the enormous buttress of the Fairweather Range to the east, crowned by fifteen thousand–foot Mt. Fairweather itself. Trailing off to the south, the spiny peaks of Chichagof and Baranof Islands gradually succumb to the curve of the Earth. Nowhere else on the planet does such grandeur pile itself so hard against the edge of the ocean, reaching these dizzying heights within a few miles of tidewater. At intervals I pause in my work, and lifting my gaze I am stunned all over again by the view that confronts me. Gratitude wells up, pushing against the silence of an inarticulate awe. I linger with the gift, letting it sink to my core, then turn again to my work.

On days like today I remember why I've come here. The clear sky and gentle swell, the steady slap and thump of blackcod as they are gaffed aboard, all contribute to a mood of pleasant engagement. Yesterday's nasty weather dissolves in an atmosphere of steady, flowing work and good-natured camaraderie, all spiced by the stupendous view. "This is almost too nice," I catch myself thinking. And even as I do so, I sense a freshening of the breeze.

A new wave of emotion touches me in the moment I become conscious of the wind, and I look around again, warily this time. Its meaning is not lost on me. The emotion I feel now is tinged with dread. As a commercial fisherman, I know that days of clarity and calm like this one are a rare event. The Gulf of Alaska is preeminently a place of tough, combative weather. The longline fisheries that bring me here take place during the time of year when equinoctial storms pound relentlessly on the gulf. The "mountains" I typically watch from this deck are built of slate gray water.

When a blow sets in, the mood changes fast, and it takes as much energy to stay on my feet as it does to do the work itself. Days are long and bone wearying, sleep short, the work tedious and dangerous. Contact with family and outside news is almost completely suspended. In these conditions, hammered by wind and sea, I sometimes feel marooned on a barren, inhospitable planet. My own inner landscape reflects these fierce contrasts. As absences grow long, and the weather mean, it takes spiritual discipline to maintain my focus and presence of mind.

There is not a season that passes without such moments of desolation, times when I question the sanity of my choice to return here. Experience tells me that the desolation will pass. Yet the question remains. Why do I persist in this work? Why have I relinquished my rights to a career in more comfortable places? In some ways, the impulse that brings me here is no different from the ancient call to the hunt that has captivated the male spirit since the Pleistocene. I can feel it rise in my blood with the spring thaw, with the return of the herring to spawn, with the increased activity and growing anticipation on the docks. As boats gear up, and old crews come back together, the memories of last year's hardships fade, and a new optimism sets in. The urge to go out one more time becomes irresistible.

But I am also driven by less noble impulses: the lure of big money, the aura of competition and conquest, the need to prove myself all over again. There is a lurking desire to pit technology against nature and win. These contradictions of modern life are not the exclusive domain of the city. They dog us to the ends of the Earth. My moods, and my musings, during these long days on the fishing grounds, bounce back and forth between these conflicting impulses; between my desire to embrace the natural world, to drink deep of these primal forces, and my desire for comfortable prosperity; between my desire to be present to this place, and my desire to conquer it; between my wish to honor these wild forces, both within me and around me, and my desire to exploit them for profit.

Every year it is harder for me to hold the contradictions in balance. Each season the doubts increase with my awareness of the damage being done to this part of the Earth's ecosystem. My forebears in this work did not enter the fishing grounds with the awesome technologies I wield, nor were they prompted by the voracious appetite of a human population run out of control. Where my predecessors in traditional cultures sought food for their families or villages to tide them through the winter, I am here to replenish my winter bank account, compressing a year's earnings into a few months. I am catching thousands of times what my personal needs warrant, and few of these fish will find their way to my table. Instead, they will travel through an elaborate processing and marketing system that will eventually carry them around the globe. And where I once could go all day without seeing another boat, I now look out on a horizon that is strewn with longliners and factory trawlers, assaulting not only the fish stocks, but the rich ocean ecosystems that sustain them. My attention ricochets back and forth between the work at hand—the tedium and challenge and exhilaration of this oceangoing craft, and my growing awareness that it is not fun anymore, it's not working, it can't go on. Worse yet, I won't escape this dilemma by going somewhere else. I'm already out on the "edge" of the Last Frontier.

This is a painful reckoning, no doubt about it. There is anguish in the thought that I am watching something die; that in my craving to be out here, to be a part of this life, I am inadvertently participating in its demise. I grieve to think that my children may not have a chance to stand here in my place, may not be able to watch this spectacle, or answer this ancient call. But I also know that I am not alone in this grieving.

What I am feeling is rapidly becoming a collective anguish, looming over the full spectrum of livelihoods, from fishing and woodworking to medicine, law, and high finance. There is no place to hide, no reasonable grounds left for denying that an ecological catastrophe of global dimensions is pending. The wounds we have inflicted on the Earth are beginning to gather us into themselves, claiming us as part of the cost. As CNN's Ted Turner has said, "It's no fun being rich on a dying planet."

This is "the pain / of the work / of wrecking the world" that poet Gary Snyder has named so aptly.[1] I am convinced it is a new breed of pain, more virulent than any that has preceded it. Since the dawn of time we have had our private griefs, our train of human sorrows. But the pain I am working with here is different. Because it grows out of unprecedented threats to our planetary life-support systems, it spills over the old ego boundaries. We cannot "resolve" it in therapy, or bury it in the psychic landfills of ever more work and money. We cannot dish it off on bureaucrats and regulators, politicians and special interest groups. We cannot look outside ourselves for the blame. The wounded Earth is itself a colossal mirror, reflecting exactly what we are doing to ourselves. No matter where we look now, we are staring into this mirror. It should not surprise us, then, to find our spirits crying out in grief and rage.

Out here on the grounds, I have plenty of time to ponder these thoughts. No phone is ringing, no TV blaring, no children clamoring for my attention. Just the incessant motion of the boat, the sting of wind and salt spray, the pungent smell of dressed blackcod. It is important to keep my mind on my work. A slack attention can be deadly when the hooks are flying out the chute, or when the strain on the fishing gear grows intense. But the skill required is a mechanical skill, and there are long spaces when I forget myself in my work, and my mind goes where it will. Sometimes lively conversation moves into these spaces. Other times no one speaks for hours, lulled by the relentless progression of work to be performed. Then the mind truly can spring loose. The opportunity for untrammeled thought is a rich by-product of this work.

And so I find myself returning to the nagging discomfort in my soul. I wince when it comes, wanting to push it away, and yet knowing I cannot. The very intransigence of the pain begins to open cracks in my thinking. One does not linger with pain indefinitely. Sooner or later I must turn to face it, and when I do, I encounter a fateful choice. Will I face the pain as an enemy or as a friend? Is it an obstacle to be overcome, or a messenger pointing the way I now must go? What are the opportunities embedded in this pain? I am clear that, for me, something profound and important is moving here. I want to hear it, to allow myself to be moved by it. Deep down in my bones, I know that the anguish I feel is a good thing. It is a useful pain. It has my attention. To embrace legitimate anguish is a healing, a cleansing thing. It opens the way to move ahead to a stronger place. And so it is now. Something new is being required of us. A new way of being in the world is beckoning. On the deepest level, this is the message I am receiving from my pain. The Earth itself is speaking through me, and I am being shaped to answer.

Where do I find the wisdom to respond? I know now that the assumptions I brought here have failed. The world is not a package of commodities, a collection of "resources" to be "harvested." The ocean does not exist for my sake. And I am not apart. This view is deadly precisely because it is "dead." The world is abundant with life, through and through, far beyond what I can see. The universe is alive!

Real wisdom starts with the realization that, as Timothy Weiskel has said, "We cannot survive in a world that we alone can imagine."[2] A natural world that is reduced to the status of "commodities" is a world of impoverished imagination. It is a "stupid" world. What I see with my human intelligence is only a tiny clearing in the forest of natural phenomenon. It is most remarkable, perhaps, for what it leaves unseen. When I am able to embrace my own immense ignorance about the natural world, to include in the loop that which I cannot myself imagine, I do not demean my intelligence, but elevate it. Only then can I see the world rightly, or wonder well at the mystery of our existence. Only then can I disarm the arrogance of what I think I know. Even here on this far northern ocean I see what this arrogance is costing us.

Clearly, a wider field of vision is called for. "Knowledge" must be opened back up to "wisdom," and wisdom must include not only things yet to be seen, but things forgotten. A configuration of consciousness beckons that is both ancient and new. As always, Gary Snyder has taught me much in this regard:

> [The] fundamental myth to which a people subscribe moves at glacial speed but is almost implacable. . . . We stand on the lateral moraine of the glacier eased along by Newton and Des-

cartes. The revivified Goddess Gaia glacier is coming down another valley, from our distant pagan past, and another arm of ice is sliding in from another angle: the no-nonsense meditation view of Buddhism with its emphasis on compassion and insight in an empty universe. Someday they will probably all converge, and yet carry streaks on each section that testify to their place of origin.[3]

I ease the boat ahead into the swell, clearing hooks and gaffing fish aboard, mesmerized by the parade of surprises that the hooks bring with them from the deep. I'm reflecting now on these glacial "streaks" as they have appeared in my own life. Trained in the classical Judeo-Christian tradition at divinity school, I tested the waters of a career in the ministry, then opted for a very different kind of life. My move to the north was a spiritual as well as a geographic leap into uncharted waters. It pushed against caution, and my very real fear of the unknown. But I resisted my impulse to go back, and for that I am grateful.

Coming to Alaska was a turning point, an important fork in the road. I sensed when I came that pieces were missing from my experience that no amount of academic study could supply. I sensed spiritual depths that my own tradition had betrayed, or forgotten. The "side glaciers" needed visiting, and this was as good a place to do that as any. I trusted that in this place, with this work, a neglected part of myself would come forth. Now, as I come around on the gear, mindful of tide and the direction of the swell, I forget that I was ever anywhere else. I know that I have found the convergence of spirit and place that I was seeking.

Ultimately, the power and magic of a place lie not in its particular features, but in our choice to inhabit it, our willingness to truly make it "home." Strictly speaking, the road could have led anywhere with similar effect. But for me it led here. There is unmistakable beauty in this lonely stretch of ocean. A dark, menacing spirit broods here as well. But the real essence of this place lies in my response to being here, in my capacity to see reflected here a measure of my own inner depth. That is the hardest part of the work, and the most important. What I seek most earnestly is knowledge of the wider, encompassing Nature that contains and upholds my human nature. With naturalist Richard Nelson, I yearn to correct "the accident of being born to a culture that separates nature and home."[4]

To my continuing surprise, that fork in the road has never led back to the highway I left behind. I have learned to love the rhythms of a life that tie me so directly to the seasons, that anchor me in the daily progression of tide and weather, anticipation and fatigue. I have come to know by experience the annual rites of hunting and fishing when the time is right for each, the satisfaction of intense physical work followed by periods of inwardness and rest. I have learned that we do not serve the world more authentically when we confine ourselves to a human social and political arena. We do not escape complicity in the depletion of natural resources by placing ourselves at the far end of the supermarket chain as anonymous consumers. And so I feel a purpose here no less valid than the one I left behind.

Precisely because I am so far from the halls of power, the centers of human culture, I am in a good place to ask the questions that now most need asking. Being in this elemental setting does much to temper the illusion that we control our destiny, that we can remake the world in our own image, with minimal reference to the ecosystems that actually uphold our life. Here I must factor into my queries the danger that lurks in this rising gale, and the fact that I am too far out on the ocean to run for cover. I must take account of the natural fear and wonder that accompanies tempestuous forces.

In the presence of so much grandeur, I see my limitations in sharper relief. This too must be factored into the questions themselves. What is the sustaining value of human culture? What gives it that value? Some places cannot be "sacred" while others are "profane." New York is not intrinsically less "natural" than the Fairweather Range. The wild forces that confront me here are alive in the city as well. They may be temporarily dormant or diminished in places where we have most crudely left our stamp. We may trick ourselves into thinking that we have banished them from the room. But we cannot. Snyder has observed that "wilderness may temporarily dwindle, but wildness won't go away. A ghost wilderness hovers over the entire planet: the millions of tiny seeds of the original vegetation are hiding in the mud on the foot of an arctic tern, in the dry desert sands, or in the wind, . . . always preserving the germ."[5] The Earth is far more patient and resilient than we have allowed ourselves to believe.

We will find a new resonance with the Earth. Only the shape of that resonance is up for grabs. We must still determine whether or not we will remain central players in the life drama of this planet. But the wild seed that is within us will go on. It does not belong to us, and we cannot destroy it. Our primary hope is not in ever larger storehouses of human knowledge, but in the wild corridors of an emerging, ever-renewing, always-sufficient natural world. We can still learn to cooperate with the Earth. Our part does not have to end here. Like the Earth itself, we are products of four billion years of evolution. The memory of that journey is recorded in every cell of our body, as it is in every niche of the created order. That memory will live in us until we are ready to hear its voice again.

That is what I am listening for. What I seek now is the courage to face the contradictions I carry within as I continue on this journey; the mindfulness to notice my fellow travelers, human and nonhuman, and take pleasure in their companionship; the willingness to feel the cold wind and sharp swell coursing through my body. I want to be here. I want my children to carry this precious seed forward. The grief that is in my heart is a messenger from that place of deep yearning. It is not unwelcome. It pulls me toward a future that can still be graced with human presence and wonder, one that is sustained by hope, and as rich with possibility as this very moment itself.

✦ *12* ✦

The Path of Place

by SHEILA KELLY

Once you find a place that feels halfway right, and it seems time, settle down with a vow not to move any more. Then taking a look at one place on Earth, one circle of people, one realm of beings over time, conviviality and maintenance will improve. . . . People begin to really notice the plants, birds, stars, when they see themselves as members of a place. . . . We look deeply back in time to the original inhabitants, and too, far ahead to our own descendants, in the mind of knowing a context. . . . Real people stay put.[1]

Poet Gary Snyder speaks in praise of "staying put" extolling the virtue of living a way that people looked on not long ago as unacceptably constrictive. Early in this century, being "tied" to a place was a limitation one sought to overcome by acquiring affluence and an automobile. And "know your place" was an exhortation to humility and deference. Then came the era of mobility madness, where moving up and moving around were the modern ways of life. But something is changing again. The prospect of staying put is gaining appeal. Tradition says that we demonstrate we are an adult person when we "settle down." Snyder is saying that in order to be a person of substance, we must, in fact settle *in*—"Real people stay put."

What happens when we settle in and sink roots? Just as the sun, soil, and rainfall combine to form the indigenous plants of a locale, we are shaped by our place. The thoughts we have, the clothes we wear, the tone of our skin, the kind of work we do, the rhythm of our lives are all affected by where we are. We interact with the people and the plants and the geography of our setting. I am drawn to meditation by the Olympic Mountains, feel solemn in the presence of Western Red Cedars, aspire to kayak the Inside Passage to Alaska, dress casually, and devote my energies to protecting the environment. My life path unfolds from being Sheila-in-Seattle. Intentionally or unintentionally, we all cocreate our lives from the interactions we have as a person-in-place. With those interactions come knowledge, joy, care, curiosity, and responsibility—which taken all together define our "sense of place."

My experience is that this sense of place feeds a deep human need and at the same time it offers hope for an emerging sense of global responsibility. As with so many other phenomena, we are giving a new name—sense of place—to an old reality. Earlier societies had no choice but to pay attention to where they were—survival of the species depended on knowing the topography, geography, the seasons, the weather, the plants, and animals. But somewhere along the way, Western religion separated humanity from the Earth and matter from spirit, while science separated truth into parts. Now we are on a great quest to rediscover connections and wholeness. With our occidental mind-set, we struggle to understand how matter and spirit are fused, even while we may intuitively grasp the reality. Experiencing the spirit of a place can bring together humanity and Earth, spirit and matter, in a new and powerful way.

As I look back, I now see that discovering and developing a personal sense of place has been my spiritual path for the last decade. I was raised in a large, devout, and loving Catholic family. I had sixteen years of Catholic education, including a degree from a Jesuit university. For me, my tradition was rich, deeply rooted, and spiritually sustaining until my thirties, which was the mid-1970s. Then over a period of several years, I became increasingly detached and disconnected. I remember the exact moment, sitting at Mass, when it became painfully clear that my spiritual life was not being nourished, but in fact was withering; and the primary reason was the way the church looked upon and ministered to women. So I left. I practiced Zen meditation for a while, and then just let go of any searching. I settled in, focusing on my work and my family, which led me to pay more attention to where I was.

My place is the Puget Sound region of western Washington state. I was born and raised in the drier, flatter, eastern part of the state and for eighteen years lived in various other regions of the United States. Then one summer I came back to my home state and "discovered" a compelling resonance with the salt water, the Cascade and Olympic Mountains, the cedars and fir, the mist, fog, and even the rain. Somehow this combination of green and gray horizons punctuated by ragged blue and white peaks, and the mossy, salty dampness fed my soul and brought me peace and energy. I won't ever move again; and I resolved to make my life's work something that honored my connection and capitalized on the energy I drew from being here.

I had been an environmental advocate by training and temperament. It was a profession that generally paid little or nothing, but I truly felt called to do it. I noticed that there were a lot of other spiritual, nonchurchgoing people who chose to serve environmental causes. I used my skills to educate and involve the public in two particular areas, energy conservation and water quality protection.

I had been living in the Northwest about five years when during one summer, four dead gray whales washed ashore on Puget Sound. The public was alarmed. I was moved. At that point, my identification with my "place" moved down from the mountaintops to include the marine depths and the ocean creatures. I was disturbed by what was happening to my fellow species. If I was truly connected to this place, then I had to do what I could to protect them all as well, not out of altruism or righteousness, but from basic self-interest. If the whales are dying, and the fish have liver tumors, and the water contains toxicants, then somehow, I too am at risk. I was moving from being an observer to being a participant.

About this time too, I heard a wetland and a whale sing. It was June and I had just finished a meeting at a suburban fire station located down the highway from a classic sprawling suburban mall. There had been great controversy over this site because it was a significant wetland. Now, even with 115 stores in place the developer wanted to expand into the last remaining piece of wetland. As I stepped out into that summer night, an amazing sound was coming from across the road—a chorus of hundreds or maybe thousands of tree frogs joined in harmonic intonation. I stood there listening, facing up the highway toward the outpouring of asphalt and molten neon that seemed poised to engulf this fragile, magical site. I knew about the need to preserve wetlands—for stormwater control and water purification, but those are the arguments of engineers. This wetland had a soul. In that instant I became a wetland advocate.

I heard Orca whales singing, too, in my living room. For vacation, our family had rented the home of a whale scientist on the west side of San Juan Island. He had placed hydrophones on a reef just out from the shore so he could watch and record the whales as part of his study to correlate their sounds and behavior. The hydrophones hooked up to the stereo speakers in the house. We ate our fresh-caught salmon dinner to the background noises of the whistles and clicks of J-Pod, (a resident group of Orcas) in pursuit of their salmon dinners. It was a kind of communion. As we finished our cobbler of freshly picked blackberries, I began to know what Wendell Berry was talking about:

> We and our country create one another, depend on one another, are literally part of one another, our land passes in and out of our bodies just as our bodies pass in and out of the land, that as we and our land are part of one another, so all who are living as neighbors here, human and plant and animal, are part of one another, and so cannot possibly flourish alone.[2]

What I have learned is that the power of place is not in the geography, topography, or any other material aspect of location. It is the spiritual communion that is somehow activated or enhanced for those who open themselves to it.

Though I may belong to the mountain and water landscape of the Pacific Northwest, there are people who draw energy from very different places, such as those who are possessed by the desert, and find nourishment in its vastness, colors, and ever-present sun. A stunning expression of this desert-mind comes from Terry Tempest Williams in *Refuge: An Unnatural History of Family and Place.*

> I believe in walking in a landscape of mirages, because you learn humility. I believe in living in a land of little water because life is drawn together. If the desert is holy, it is because it is a

forgotten place that allows us to remember the sacred. Perhaps that is why every pilgrimage to the desert is a pilgrimage to the self. There is no place to hide, and so we are found.[3]

Ms. Williams, a third-generation Mormon who grew up near the Great Salt Lake Desert, is acknowledging the profound spiritual power the desert holds for her. She experiences it as sacred. She has embraced her place; and her life as writer and naturalist demonstrates what can be done when you "bloom where you are planted."

It is not only pristine beauty and wilderness that capture the heart, but some mystery that connects people to certain environments. I once watched a woman get off the plane and kiss the flat, dusty ground of Ada, Oklahoma, grateful to be out of those claustrophobic Rocky Mountains!

What happens with this heightened awareness of place? My first feeling is of being privileged to live here. Then I feel gratitude— gratitude to the Creator of this magnificence. To me, this creation is compelling evidence of divine intelligence, goodness, beauty, and love. This is not an uncommon response in the Pacific Northwest. Washington state may have the nation's lowest church membership, but many of those folks spending Sundays taking a walk, scaling a mountain, or kayaking in the Sound just for the love of it, know it is also a spiritual exercise. Taken collectively, this is a worship service, acknowledging the Creator through celebration of the sacredness of creation.

The potential for this spiritual connection is there, almost anywhere, for those who stay put and pay attention. An elder of the Crow Tribe reassures us: "You know, I think if people stay somewhere long enough—even white people—the spirits will begin to speak to them. It's the power of the spirits coming up from the land. The spirits and the old powers aren't lost, they just need people to be around long enough and the spirits will begin to influence them."[4]

According to Snyder, long enough is four hundred years. "That's how long it takes to make enough observations about where we are to live there respectfully, in harmony with all the other members of the animal and plant community."

Not many of us think in terms of four hundred years, making

decisions with "the seventh generation" in mind, as Native American tradition counsels. I've only been on this path of place twelve years now. I know it is the mountains and tree frogs, whales and blackberries, wetlands and salmon that ground me and bring me such great joy. I also know I can't stop with my own personal sense of satisfaction.

After awareness and gratitude comes responsibility. I am called to care for and protect that which gives me joy. Once again it is paying attention—to ensure that how I live is in harmony with where I live. For me, as a householder, it can be simple everyday choices like finding substitutes for toxic cleaners, or not dumping motor oil in the storm drain. It's watching my use of pesticides and solvents. As a citizen, it is monitoring policies and activities that could potentially degrade the environment. As a professional, I chose to apply my skills working for a state agency focused on the cleanup and protection of Puget Sound.

This agency developed an education program that assumed that the environmental ethic needed to clean up and protect Puget Sound would only emerge from peoples' discovery or development of a sense of place. For many, "water quality" was an obscure concept, and even Puget Sound was an abstraction. But people knew their bay or neighborhood stream, and they cared about whether or not the clams were safe to eat and the salmon were returning to spawn. Beginning with the concern for a part, people begin to see how their immediate environment is connected to larger systems. Then the idea of watersheds, land-based sources of pollution, cumulative impacts, and individual and collective responsibility become relevant.

As we learn about and care for our chosen place, we know it is only a part of a larger whole—a city, a county, a state, a region, a continent, a planet. We share the air and the water that flow through all these parts of a global system. Puget Sound is affected by what happens in British Columbia—by the quality of the fish habitat in the Fraser River and the forest practices on Vancouver Island. As much as we may want to withdraw to take solace and joy and live in harmony in our own place, we are linked. Inevitably we must come to the larger question: How do we ground human cultures within natural systems?

This larger question has given rise to a whole new body of thought—bioregionalism. People are looking more closely both at how their communities relate to nature and how the community interacts with its locale. Again this is the rediscovery of an organizing principle that operated for centuries:

> Bioregionalism is an idea still in loose and amorphous formulation, and presently [it] is more hopeful declaration than actual practice. . . . Hardly a new notion, it has been the animating cultural principle through 99 percent of human history.[5]

Bioregions are defined by watersheds, drainage patterns, plant and animal species. If you ask Gary Snyder where he lives, he would respond, "On the western slope of the northern Sierra Nevada, in the Yuba River Watershed, north of the south fork at the three-thousand-foot elevation, in a community of Black Oak, Incense, Cedar, Madrone, Douglas Fir, and Ponderosa Pine."[6]

Bioregionalism assumes that there is a direct connection between the health of natural systems and our own physical/psychic health as individuals and as a species. So it was no surprise that the first North American Bioregional Congress (1984) issued a call to activism:

> A growing number of people are recognizing that in order to secure the clean air, water and food that we need to healthfully survive, we have to become guardians of the places where we live. . . . The best way to take care of ourselves . . . is to protect and restore our region.[7]

This kind of consciousness will determine the future. It brings formerly complacent people out to testify at hearings or stand in front of bulldozers to defend the land or trees, to demonstrate their sense of solidarity with a region. "Bioregionalism is the entry of place into the dialectic of history."[8]

While we consider the blessings and responsibilities connected to these places where we live and our bioregion, we too, must move from the part to the whole. When the Apollo astronauts presented us with moon rocks and a photograph of Earth from space, the definition of place and bioregion changed forever. Now we are called to cultivate a commensurate sense of ownership and account-ability for our home planet.

In grappling with this global imperative, people respond in ways that range from mundane to monumental. From buttons and bumper stickers—"Love Your Mother," and "Good Planets Are Hard to Find,"—to the 1992 United Nations Earth Summit in Rio de Janeiro, where one hundred seventy-eight nations gathered to deliberate on the world's future.

I have my share of buttons and bumper stickers, but I felt a need for more information and exposure to the complex international issues that arise when many peoples in many places attempt to interact as a whole system. So, over a two-year period, I partici-pated in the Earth Summit preparations and Conference. My intent was to learn how to "think global" after my twenty years of acting local. I wanted a deeper understanding of how place and planet fit together. It was an intentional practice, not unlike a Zen discipline, on my Path of Place. As it turned out, the Earth Summit was a profound personal experience, and a test of my capacity and will-ingness to expand my own awareness, gratitude, and sense of re-sponsibility to a global context.

After Rio, my awareness must include not only those gray whales that died for unknown reasons in Puget Sound, but also the thirty-five thousand children who die of diarrhea every day for lack of clean water and basic health care; and as I bless the rain that falls on my greening garden, I know that desertification is ravaging Africa. I cannot excape the conclusion that if we are to "protect and restore our bioregion" that ultimately is the planet, then we have to con-front consumption, militarism, debt, population, and poverty, along with toxic wastes, polluted oceans, ozone depletion, forests, and all the other concerns.

My expanded awareness has brought less denial and more pain. How can I still feel gratitude? What's to keep me from succumbing to the world media assertion that the conference accomplished little and, as usual, pollution and politics prevailed? Many things kept me from that terminal pessimism. On my way to Rio I visited the Amazon, and along a dark jungle stream, an iridescent sky-blue butterfly six inches across flew right over my head. It had the same effect on me as hearing the tree frogs in the Northwest wetland. I was grateful for that dazzling moment, a reminder that the Amazon has a soul and that the spirit of this place too must be honored. In Rio, I was inspired by the stories of courageous women from Africa and India who were putting their lives in danger as they worked to reforest their country or stop construction of a dam that would wipe out a culture. It was all a reminder that amidst the cynicism and destruction being documented for the Earth Summit, there were always moments of beauty and hope. Just as in my native Northwest, it was that combination of beauty and the threat of degradation that triggers a sense of responsibility.

My responsibility now is to declare and demonstrate that every local act is a global act. In every locus around the world, from Puget Sound to the Sahara Desert, what we do in our own place— the way we live, consume, pollute, or preserve—is affecting a global system that affects all the people of the planet. We must demand the building of a *global* community with values different from today's international institutions that are based on fiercely guarded national sovereignty. The world community must proceed with a true conviction that we are all inextricably linked through our shared humanity and our dependence on those shared natural systems— water, air, soil—which support all life on this planet.

Perhaps my responsibility doesn't stop even there, and my path of place asks more. This occurred to me as I pondered an incident at the United Nations in New York, when I was wandering around between sessions of the Earth Summit preparatory meetings. I came upon a display case housing an intriguing crystal pyramid. When I looked closer, I saw it contained the rocks brought to Earth by the Apollo astronauts who landed on the moon February 4, 1971. I remember standing at the case a long time, awed by the thought that these nondescript gray chunks had come from a distant, unknown, alien origin. But in my journal I had noted only that the rocks "looked like something I might pick up from a beach in Puget Sound." Although totally outside my realm of experience, my response to these exotic objects was one of recognition. There is a connection between my beach and a moon crater. This path I am on is teaching me that bioregion and planet are still only part of a yet larger Place.

✦ *13* ✦

Moonlight Glistening
on the Water

by DAVID GUNDERSON

One evening in November, as the last light of dusk faded into night, the moon rose from behind the Cascades, full and golden. Niles, my five-year-old son, and I stepped out onto the porch to watch. Soon after, as we were driving down the hill near our house, I saw the moon reflected in the water of Commencement Bay and said, "Oh, Niles, look! I love the moonlight glistening on the water." He saw too, and said with excitement, "So do I!" Then softly, to himself, he repeated the word: "Glistening . . . glistening."

What happened in the car that night was at the heart of human culture: a little boy learning language with his father. It was the best kind of education, a process of formation guided by love. But it was not only our love for each other that guided us that night. We also shared our love for the moon, and for the sense of presence it awakened in us. We were excited, stirred to speech by the wonder of finding ourselves alive in this great mystery.

I hope my son will never lose his sense of communion with this living world, the communion in which a glistening on the water becomes the "glistening" of his mind. I hope that he will always see the beauty of human ordering, and know that he is also a shining presence in the world. I hope that he will feel the depth of his belonging, and remember that he is included in that oldest benediction: "And God saw everything which had been made, and behold, it was very good."

I know he will be tempted to forget these deepest truths about himself and the world. In time he will see the darkness and contradictions of our human presence on the Earth. He will experience them for himself, in his own heart. He will understand the extent to which we are all implicated in the very suffering we seek to overcome.

My dilemma as a father is that, while I fear his encounter with suffering, I know also that he will lose himself and the world if he tries to avoid it. The glistening will fade if he turns away from knowledge. I cannot, then, indulge in the false hope that he might somehow be spared this awakening. I pray instead for the safety of his heart, that he might live in the place of clear-sighted love and return this gift of sight to the world for its healing.

I hope my son's life overflows with love, given and received, even though I know that love is accompanied by pain. There is no other way. Suffering is inevitable when we love, when we choose to honor our relatedness to the world, without denials or betrayal, without turning away. The human vocation is to persist in love, to allow the circle of our communion to widen rather than constrict, until everything and everyone is included. Only then will we have become ourselves, knowing the depth of our belonging to the whole of creation.

A Native Elder Speaks: How Do You Say Good-bye to a Friendship?

by KEN COOPER

I walked in the lush undergrowth of the old-growth trees, prayed to them and for them. A gentle breeze drifted through and in these trees, the ones we call the "standing people." Far away I could hear words of the old ones saying to stop the destruction of the Earth, all things are connected. The streams babbling through the mountains are like blood flowing in your veins, the rivers like arteries carrying the gift of blood of the heart. We the true people of this land have cried to the four directions over and over, saying the same things. People listen but don't hear, they are spiritually malnourished, no feelings for Mother Earth!

I have tried to show a common boundary by traveling and speaking on behalf of Mother Earth. Playing the songs of the old ones to empty ears, playing the old-growth cedar flute songs of the wind. People are listening but not hearing! How can one impart spirituality to empty souls?

Our people have had a long and satisfying friendship with the "standing people," giving and taking on both parts! When I look into paper that once was a tree, and see all the elements that come from within, I see laws that mean nothing to the ones who enforce them. By their law, if you take a life you lose your own. If you rape, you lose your freedom. By their laws anything you do can jeopardize your freedom. But when it comes to the land and all things that live here, the home of the true people, the law is not in affect! Kill the trees, destroy the homes of the animal people, the birds. Everything there is the friend of my people, and there is no place to go to say good-bye to them. Once gone they are gone forever. If I lose a friend I go to the cemetery to say good-bye. No matter how I lose someone or something there is a way to say good-bye to it or them. But I speak of losing a friendship where there is no place or way to say good-bye. As I sit and write of this they are cutting trees, damming rivers, and all that they do they keep doing!

They have built a bridge between us, a strong bridge of mistrust, and paved this bridge with broken treaties or promises. My aunts and uncles were taken away and their hair cut off, they were beaten for speaking our language. Our masks and regalia were burned, our totem pole destroyed, our homes taken away, and we were made to move onto reservations. We were made to sell the food we eat, our fish and all seafood, in order to pay rent and electricity bills. We were made to send our children to schools eight hours a day, being taught by white teachers, given medicines from a bottle instead of from the forest. They are eating our traditions because they have none of their own! And when they fill themselves they still won't have any!

How do you say good-bye to a friendship?

My life is drifting to the winter portion of its time and I look back and see no accomplishments. I fought and let them know I was here and when I leave no one will even know I existed. For we are but a grain of sand on life's beach and throw us into the water and we make but a small ripple! Before I leave this world and enter into another I need to know how to say good-bye to a friendship.

My canoe will be passing, and I will ride this canoe regardless of where it will go. A wild ride ahead of me? Or an easy one? I will ride it out, for I walked and left a few tracks, maybe not as a lot of people would have liked me to walk, but I was here.

I throw my breath to the four winds, I thank my four grandparents from where I come. I pray to the ones that gave me this life, and to my Creator I give thanks for this small life I live, and for the friends I met on this journey.

I will soon go to have twenty-one trails smoothed out for me, and now I will have to trust in the ones I speak against, to use their healing on me, because our Indian doctors live no more. And there is no place left to go and fast for these gifts any more, for they have been cut down, buildings or something placed on top of them. So now I pray to the Father of all, to guide my mind, my soul, and my being to trust in them.

I have had a good friendship with my self over the years. I say not good-bye. I say we will cross paths again. If not I will send a great canoe, I will carve it myself from the silver lining of the place my Father laid out for me.

I rode the thunder, walked the rainbows, shook hands with lightning, I now ride the winds, my flute plays the love songs of my heart, my drum beats the rhythm of life itself into the heart of hearts that pounds out this song.

The mountains call my name, CHA-DAS-SKA-DUM.

I'm the image of my self, I'm the Indian.

✦ *15* ✦

Environment and Religion: The Evolution of a New Vision

by The Very Reverend
JAMES PARKS MORTON

In this, the last decade of the twentieth century, there has been a radical change in the way in which we view creation—the Earth, its inhabitants, its faiths, the church—the very foundation of our beliefs. If there were one moment from which we can date this change, it would be on the day in the year 1969 when the first photographs of the Earth as seen from the moon were released.

That image of astonishing and singular beauty, that azure aquamarine orb, out there in the dark vastness of space, shimmering against the void, transformed forever how we view the planet we call home. It has become the metaphor and icon for a new way of thinking about religion and about life in the twenty-first century. The glory of the photograph from the moon is that it is a symbol of unity containing complexity, not just a white circle on a black field but, indeed, a blue and green and brown and white globe, a figured, textured, riveted, peaked, and turning unity, infinitely complex and yet one.

The moon shot symbolized the new thinking that had begun to capture many of our finest minds—in science, philosophy, the arts, religion. It caught the imagination with its beauty. It also offered a challenge . . . the challenge both to recognize the sacred in that orb and to respond to the threat that humankind's profligacy, care-lessness, and greed posed to its continued existence. To make the sacredness of *all* creation the focus and font of religion—that is the challenge.

The challenge for the Christian church was/is to reform its thinking so that it is centered on the revelation embodied in that image. After all, the word *religion* itself, etymologically, means "to bind together." And so, as we humans discovered the fragility of the environment, we began to focus on ecology, the science of the relationships between organisms and their environments. The word *ecology* is derived from the roots for home and knowledge—*oikos* (house, about the house) and *logos* (the word, reckoning, thought). Thus, at the heart of the ecological sciences is *housekeeping;* keep your house clean, love it, tend it, serve it, care for it—your house, your home. Earth. *And* ecology is about the interrelatedness, the sacred interrelatedness, of all things. Ecology, in this sense, has renewed or confirmed religious insight and understanding.

For me the awareness of the environmental crisis and the importance of ecology nearly coincided with becoming dean of the Cathedral of St. John the Divine in 1972.

The environment was not always at the center of my ministry. In the early years—in the dock areas of Jersey City and in inner city Chicago—my activities and those of others in the forefront of the religious community focused on issues of poverty and social justice and, in the global realm, peace and disarmament. Our models were the French worker-priests. I didn't even know the word *ecology.* Shortly after coming to the Cathedral I was introduced to a remarkable group of people—philosophers, chemists, biologists, physicists, poets, artists, theologians—through William Irwin Thompson, who asked me to be part of the newly forming Lindisfarne Association. These included Gregory Bateson, John Todd, Nancy Jack-Todd, and Fritz Schumacher. Enlightened by their perceptions, I began to look at creation from a new perspective.

A major shift for me came when Rene Dubos and Thomas Berry entered my sphere in 1975. In fact, my understanding of the universe, of humanity's relationship to the Earth as it had been spelled out in the Judeo-Christian tradition, was reconceptualized. A radical transformation occurred. The questions: how does science function? how do art and literature function? how does religion function? were old, but the vision was new. Since that time my task has been to put flesh on this skeletal reconception; to speak it, yes, but also to act it out, to make it living and palpable, to *experience* it in every aspect of Cathedral life.

Now, a cathedral is by definition a sort of microcosm, as all the great holy places of the world are and always have been. A pyramid, a parthenon, a synagogue, a mosque, a cathedral, each sacred site in its very physical and conceptual scale is a center of thought, the arts, and commerce. It stands as the hub of the whole *community.* Great holy places are always found at the center, for they are related to everything that goes on in society. Humankind's understanding of its place in the cosmos is raised to its highest expression in its sacred sites. The French term, used by Rene Dubos, captures the meaning: *haut lieu* (a high place) whether it's the mountain itself or the temple on the mount. Obviously, then, as an understanding of religion evolves, the role of its institutions, of the cathedral, must evolve, too. A whole new lexicon, language, and metaphor must be created for it to remain in sync with the profound comprehension of the world and the place of people in it. As dean, I have always tried to guide the Cathedral to reflect the richest and most evolved thinking about God's creation.

And an awakening has happened! In the score of years since 1972, a great realignment, a new place in the sun, a shift in the universe, in the understanding of creation has begun to emerge beneath the Cathedral's vaults. This shift represents no less than a rift in the so-called civilized world with the generations of the past and even with our grandparents, but it has also established a solidarity with indigenous people worldwide, and especially with our own Native American brothers and sisters.

The Cathedral has been, and hopefully will remain, in the vanguard of this new thinking. When we at St. John's began to examine our beliefs, 99 percent of the people and leaders of religious communities—and you can name any tradition—were simply not thinking that way. Ecological insights, new paradigms and the like were a foreign language. The most advanced "religious thinking" was concerned with social action, social justice, and peace issues. When I began to point out that these very same social problems are a *part* of a larger environment that includes the globe and the universe, my religious compadres would shake their heads.

We persisted. During the decade of the 1970s the Cathedral family responded to these challenges and began the process of profound change. Dubos, Thompson, the Todds, Amory and Hunter Lovins, and Thomas Berry, all spoke from the pulpit, and I sought to restructure the given seasons of the Church to reflect the evolving understanding of the sacred. Lent, for example is very much about penitence and suffering. So, I said, "Let's talk about the suffering of the *Earth*. Let's talk about Jesus *in* Earth, God incarnate in the flesh of Earth. Let's speak of the pain of the Earth, the passion of water, the *passion of creation*." People who listened heard the message and began to understand.

In 1979 we were ready to *manifest* our comprehension. The Cathedral held its first Sun Day Celebration. Margaret Mead, Robert Redford, and Gus Speth spoke. Thousands of people came. That same year we had a huge fair on behalf of all of the environmental groups in New York. We hosted the annual four-day meeting of cathedral deans of North America (as well as half a dozen English deans) and had Tom Berry, Rene Dubos, and the Todds on hand to present their new ways of looking at the universe. New York soon got the message that we were leaders in a new environmental activism, and that word was carried by speakers and exhibits to churches and parishes throughout the continent.

Nineteen seventy-nine was a watershed year for other reasons. That was the year when James Lovelock's *Gaia: A New Look at Life on Earth* was published. Lovelock gave the first public exposition of the Gaia hypothesis from the pulpit of St. John's, the first in a series of sermons that concluded with my sermon on "Earth as God's Body," in which I tried to reconstruct theology in order to locate within Christian life the heart of the response to the new vision of Earth and the responsibility of the human species to it. We were talking about nothing less than what *it means to be religious* today.

In the summer of that momentous year, Lewis Thomas's *The Lives of a Cell* was on my reading list. Among the many profound delights of that book, I was very much taken by his description of the wart. These structures are among nature's oddities. Under the microscope they have what appears to be an impregnable defensive design. And yet, the wart can spring up overnight and is subject to the power of suggestion. The wart can be thought away! This fact has not only been demonstrated anecdotally over the centuries, but has been documented in scientifically controlled experiments. Again and again.

Thomas's ruminations over the disappearing acts of warts verge on the theological, and the point that this marvelous doctor drives home is the same as found in St. Paul: not only is the body a great mystery, such that the more we know, the infinitely greater amount we discover we have yet to learn, but the body is also the *key* to everything we know. We know the world by and through the analogies we make from our own flesh. Even our faith is defined by corporal metaphor: Jesus is the Word made Flesh; because Christ shared our flesh and blood he shares his salvation with us.

These bodily analogies can be carried even farther. The English physicist and lay theologian John Wren-Lewis reminds us that the ancient Talmudic commentaries speak of the original human person *Adam-Kadman* as having the *entire cosmos within one body:* all the galaxies and the stars within, as without. St. Paul repeats this image in the *Corpus Christi,* and most Westerners have no difficulty in applying this concept to other people. In fact, Christians think of the Church as people—men and women—the first fruits of the new creation, renewed in Christ. But something went wrong in the development of the Western church. It simply didn't follow St. Paul faithfully. Somehow the sense of *all* creation—the whole Earth, the universe, transfigured and made new in Christ—was lost (except, of course, among the mystics such as Francis of Assisi or William Blake).

It is not surprising, therefore, that what *wasn't* considered part of the body of Christ was just "stuff," even if it was beautiful stuff: stars, clouds, mountains, oceans, and trees; or even precious stuff: gold, rubies, diamonds, oil, uranium. It was all regarded as stuff, and was not deemed holy creation in the sense that human beings were considered holy. Given this fact, it was perhaps inevitable that Western civilization ended up looking upon the Earth as basically there to be used . . . source material, real estate for speculation. Didn't God, in fact, instruct his people to "be fruitful and multiply, and fill the Earth and subdue it; and have dominion over the fish of the sea and over the birds of the air and every living thing that moves upon the Earth?" We forgot that *dominion* has its root in *dominus*—dweller in the house or caretaker, the Latin equivalent of the *oikos* in ecology.

Similarly, we have tended to justify our historical path theologically; we have called people who reverence the Earth "primitive." So much for the Native American traditions. Or we've called them "pagan." So much for the sacred groves of ancient Greece or modern Africa. When it comes to China and Japan, civilizations we can hardly dismiss as primitive, where Taoist underpinnings indeed reflect a people who regard nature as sacred, well, we said, the Orient is the Orient—different, inscrutable.

Thus, the Earth was, at least in the West, simply omitted from our perceptions of the sacred and holy, and this fact has had two tremendously important results: one, good, and one, catastrophic.

The good result has been the development of Western science and technology. The modern world as we know it developed the way it did, and with the speed it did, because there were virtually no taboos nor inhibitions to slow up research and exploration. Few, if any, thought it necessary to ask the fundamental question: does the Earth have rights? Certainly, there were environmentalists and ecologists and conservationists, and even the occasional consumer advocate, who raised voices of concern about the toxicity of water and air, the long-term danger to living cells from preservatives, medicines, and chemicals, the increasing extinction of *species* of wildlife and, most frightening of all, the virtual exhaustion of topsoil in many parts of the world through ignorant or willful misuse and chemo-"therapy" along with life-threatening contamination of oceans. But these wise ones went largely unheeded. Unbridled growth began to suggest unstoppable destruction.

To me, however, the truly catastrophic result, which concerns all of us *and* the Church, is far less obvious because, frankly, it is spiritual. It is the *cumulative result that centuries of "manhandling"* the Earth has had upon our bodies, our brains, our minds, our hearts, upon the way we think and feel. Or rather, upon the way we have *ceased* to think and have become incapable of feeling. We have become spiritually barren and our capacities for sensitive response to the Earth and to each other has atrophied from disuse.

This is a fundamental, spiritual tragedy. As we at the Cathedral gained awareness, we increasingly sounded the alarm.

In 1979 we raised the banner of ecological crisis and, in 1980, joined the crucial issue of world peace to the environmental crisis, and brought political scientists, economists, biologists, nuclear regulators, philosophers, ecologists in succession onto the same stage, the same pulpit, to increase our knowledge of and commitment to change. All spoke about the energy of the Earth and the peace of the Earth in their own, so to speak, "laboratory" language; and they made an impact.

I took that theme—the religious, political, artistic importance, and significance of all environmental concerns, of our responsibility to God's creation—on the road in 1980. I would begin my talk by unrolling two posters . . . first, our icon, planet Earth as seen from space; then, a photograph of the Cathedral rose window. My point was that the two images are the same: the Earth from space reveals the sacredness of our planet; the rose window is a dramatic and radiant sacred image of the unity of creation shot through with God's glory. Until and unless we can come to see how they are related, how Earth and the rose window are part of the ecology of creation, we will never really come to grips with the environment, with world peace, with religion, with our neighbors, with ourselves.

It may seem surprising, but scientists, not theologians, were the first to comprehend the essence of these interrelationships. Rene Dubos, the microbiologist, ecologist, writer, and Christian, the wise one so crucial to the formation of my thinking, who preached at the Cathedral many times before his death, said to me on more than one occasion, with great passion and simplicity: "The scientists and the environmentalists and the politicians cannot prevent us from destroying the Earth: *only the Church can save the Earth.*" Only the Church can make people see that our feet are on holy ground— ground so holy that Moses took off his shoes.

To grasp the need to take off our shoes, to take dominion seriously as caretakers of God's creation, humanity must first understand, see, taste, touch, and feel the need to change and, in fact, to be converted. The Greek word for conversion, *repentance (metanoia),* literally means "turning around," from facing west, say, to facing east. We have to do a turn-around in our minds, as keepers of the faith, whether priest or worshipper. The questions stay the same, resounding through the ages, but the form of our response is shaped by our placement in time and space. What is it to be faithful? To lead Christian lives? To think and do what is truly right? The answers today must reflect the belief that *peacekeeping and Earth-keeping are inseparable from faith-keeping.*

Whether we speak of peace and disarmament, or energy conservation, or rainforest preservation; whether we talk about the kind of food we eat, or the temperature to which we heat our homes, the use of public transportation to reduce fuel consumption and air pollution, or the recycling of refuse, we are talking about the day-to-day decisions of how we lead a Christian life. The *way* we are religious is the issue. We are talking about Christ's message of peace, which is the essence of all that is sacred, but we are applying it to all of creation. It is really that simple: the *way* we keep the peace and the *way* we keep the Earth are the *way* we are religious.

To *live* in this new way of being religious requires *metanoia,* a turn-around of comprehension and commitment such that we know that *peace, ecology, religion* are a threefold unity and an expression of love. This is the Christian love that I have come to believe and have tried to practice in my own life and in the life of the Cathedral. This unity of belief and expression has now spread within the religious community and larger society, in this country and abroad, and is represented in a wide variety of faiths. Many practitioners of the sacred have come to believe that you cannot be religious and not be concerned about peace; you cannot be religious and not be concerned about the Earth; you cannot be religious and not wish to cherish and preserve all of God's creation. If you are not concerned about your sister/brother Earth, you are not, in fact, loving your neighbor.

Now these words, *ecology, peace, religion,* are simple, discrete, and comprehensive, but their *expression* is not. Creation is not static—not in its macrocosmic manifestation, not in its microscopic order. It involves stasis and kinesis, chaos and constancy, introversion and extrusion, consciousness and oblivion, integration and disintegration, cosmos and atom—whether we are speaking of the universe, human relations, the wing of a butterfly, or the eye of a hurricane. All, all dichotomies that direct and diffuse and dismay and delight us are part of this world in which we live, a part of Earth's Sacred Voyage.

At root for me, if God exists at all, then God, no matter how we speak of God, must be recognizable everywhere and in everything. God is in the pulse and heart, neurons and ganglia, in the liver and gizzard, and in the subatomic DNA code of everything. God *is* in everything, and that is why it is sacred, that is why it is Christian.

Tom Berry has said it: "The human is less a *being* on the Earth or in the universe than a *dimension* of the Earth and indeed of the universe itself." To see humankind thus takes a great imaginative leap. It is in this leap that we begin to recognize that all creation is present in Earth's Sacred Voyage.

One of the ways in which we at the Cathedral have tried to manifest this understanding is in recalling the life of one who embodies this vision. Each year since 1985, on the first Sunday in October, the Cathedral has held a celebration in the name of St. Francis of Assisi. Each year we sing the *Missa Gaia*, the *Earth Mass*, written and performed by Cathedral colleague Paul Winter, and conclude with an amazing procession of life—from blue-green algae to the elephant—that mounts the steps and proceeds down the nave to receive the bishop's blessing.

The celebration of St. Francis is a great occasion in our yearly calendar. This amazing spectacle serves to spotlight and remind us of the underlying unity of the Earth and our responsibility to it, and it embodies what I think of as a sort of first rule in what I call my Spiritual/Ecological Handbook of Good Housekeeping. That first rule of life on Sacred Earth is universal: *we all dwell in one house, we are all in "The Ark" together.* Because of this, our unity comes first. Our diversity as humans and other living species, every rock and rill of creation, occurs *within the unity,* so that anything that divides, that labels, that sets apart the expressions of Creation is misguided and just plain wrong.

The second spiritual rule of ecology in our Handbook is the shadow of the first. If the first rule is universal, calling upon us to recognize the face of the Lord behind each creature in Earth's community, *the second is the response to the astonishing diversity within the universe.* This cosmic diversity is such that much remains unknown to humankind. Nevertheless, we do know that each individual differs from every other: every star from every other star, every cell from every other cell, every plant from every other plant, every rock from every other rock, every species from every other species, every individual starfish, whale, wolf, or human is different from every other. So rule number one says that Christ the Lord is in every creature and we share universal kinship. Rule number two says that we are all different, radically different, and that difference is as much a part of creation as is unity.

Rule number three in our Handbook states that the condition, the modus operandi of diversity living in unity—how particulars interact with universals—is *the essence of interdependence, of indwelling, of cooperation and symbiosis* within a given organism, within a family, community, or world. We are all connected to one another, our very existence is interdependent, *we need each other to survive.* This interrelationship has been highlighted in the past decade by the Gaia hypothesis, first put forth by James Lovelock, but echoed by the work of Lynn Margulis, John Todd, Rene Dubos, and many others. They have postulated that the planet Earth, Gaia, *is alive.* The Earth, the body of Earth, and thus of Christ, is a living, breathing reality. And as the Earth is stardust, we all are stardust.

Now it is obvious to me that when we do not accept and apply rule three, the rule of our interdependence, "things fall apart, pure anarchy is loosed." This is where we humans have failed so utterly and religion, which should be the cosmic glue holding us together, has served instead as the builder of walls that keep us apart. Muslims over here, all ten branches; Buddhists over there, all twenty branches; Jews over there, but Sephardim upstairs and Ashkenazi downstairs. Christians over here, all nine hundred fighting brands. Let's throw race into the mix: blacks, there; high yellows, over there, Orientals apart—don't mix with the yellows of African descent. Gays to the left, straights to the right. Bankers, doctors, unionists, artists, teachers, keypunchers, geneticists, find your places; but women, don't mix, your place is over there. Animals to zoos. Long live the ghetto—false religion's noblest shrine. And the eye *has* said to the foot, "I have no need of you." What fools humans have been when it is so clear that we are all interdependent! All of us are a-sail on Good Ship Earth's Sacred Journey.

This ship on which we travel carries all of God's creatures. We must remember that God through Christ has taught us that our unity, our diversity, and our interdependence apply especially to the "least of these," to the hungry, the woman behind bars, the disabled man, the abused child, the thirsty, the deranged, the homeless, the *auslander*, the boat person, the victim of AIDS, the refugee. The last will be first. It is in suffering, in the place of disaster, of failure, of shame, that the greatest revelation of *God as love* can be found.

It is clear, therefore, that we must share. We must share in the times of ease and beauty, and must share in the times of disaster and tragedy. Tom Berry has said the era in which we live must be "The Age of Ecology," of communion, the time when the different galactic ages and species and peoples will dwell together as one great holy reality. Or perish.

The sum of the rules that make up my Spiritual/Ecological Handbook are both simple and truly revolutionary, and with revolution comes a profound challenge. We must re-create our role as caretakers of creation to include the nurture and preservation of *all* life through interdependence and sharing. Humanity must take responsibility through science, through the arts, through religion, to care for the sacred universe. We must love, cherish, and protect the Earth as mother of all life, of God's creation, God's light, God's love. This is the challenge in this deep enterprise. We must probe the heights and depths, we must absorb science, and then acquaint and align ourselves with issues of public policy. We must take the steps that insure change, revolution, and renewal.

At the Cathedral in the 1970s we took the first steps, we heard the voices of those who recognized and promoted a realignment of faith; we began to believe in and to practice the new vision of our responsibility. Then, in the early 1980s we linked environmental and ecological concerns to issues of social justice, peace, disarmament, and personal freedom. In the late 1980s, we began not only to preach these things but to put them into practice in forms that would reach beyond our immediate surroundings. And we sought to join with others who were carrying the message.

In December 1989, a group of thirty-four prominent scientists, led by Carl Sagan, sent out a call, which said in part that in order to succeed "efforts to safeguard and cherish the environment need to be infused with a vision of the sacred." What was especially intriguing to me was the source of the call. Science had already helped us to see the full power of the environmental challenge, but here were those who had been in the forefront of much of Western thinking for over three centuries—physicists, mathematicians, chemists, biologists, astronomers—reaching out to the community of the spirit with the message they must work together. As a result of this call, the newly formed Joint Appeal in Religion and Science convened a "Summit on the Environment" in June 1991 . . . at the Cathedral. Top leaders of major American faith groups met with distinguished scientists and with senators Al Gore and Timothy Wirth. This was the beginning of a commitment that is growing in numbers, strength, and vision.

The following summer, 1992, the Joint Appeal met in Washington, and this time fifty heads of religious denominations and fifty top scientists sat with a joint congressional committee and other high government officials. We spoke and they listened. In my testimony I told them to keep in mind that we were talking about what it means to *be religious,* now and tomorrow and henceforth. That the environmental challenge—what it reveals and what it calls for—will profoundly affect the nature of this planet and the nature of all life on it.

We told them that, for us, social justice and environmental integrity are inseparable conditions for one another; that ecological deterioration has a profound impact upon the poor and upon workers and especially upon minority peoples. We pledged that ours is and will continue to be a scholarly response, touching on theology and ethics, engaged with economists as well as ecologists. It is and will continue to be a worshipful response, upheld throughout this nation in congregations where people now pray for wetlands and endangered species, for afflicted soil and polluted air, as well as for the sick and dying and the oppressed and victims of racism. It is and will continue to be an effort to put into practice what we preach: habits of sustainable living and purchasing and investing. We told them that the Cathedral of St. John the Divine had opened Upper

Manhattan's first recycling center in the 1970s and it is still operating today. Our response is and will continue to be a pastoral response, for a response to a crisis of such magnitude and penetration takes time, requires growth and change, and must address the fear of change. Finally, we told the congressional committee that ours will always be a diverse response, that the issue of environmental integrity and justice cuts across traditional religious lines. We told them that today a consensus exists at the highest levels over a significant spectrum of religious traditions and that the urgent cause of environmental integrity must occupy a position of utmost priority for people of faith.

If the Washington testimony by the Joint Appeal represents recognition within the government establishment of this country, there was, for the health of this planet, an even more momentous occurrence in the summer of 1992. In June, with thousands of others, I went to Rio de Janeiro, Brazil, to participate in the UN Conference on Environment and Development (UNCED). The experience of those days was extraordinary, for Rio was the first time *ever* that representatives of nations throughout the world—heads of governments, leaders of science and industry, and spokespersons for many peoples and many faiths—came together to raise the issue of the environment. *The environmental crisis is now on the agenda.* Until four years ago, most people had never heard of an ozone layer, global warming, toxicity of water, dying oceans. All these things were there before we saw them, and could even be found in the back pages of some newspapers, but they were not on the church agenda, or the media agenda, not in the school curricula, nor listed on government schedules. Now that has changed forever. The environment is on the agenda.

Think of it! Even though it has been thirty years since Rachel Carson first set forth her profound ideas about the fragility and interrelatedness of all life on this planet, it is only now that the message has been heard by those who can and must respond. Only in the summer of 1992 did the world's nations, rich and poor, from five continents and many kinships join together to proclaim humankind's determination to mobilize to save our sacred home, Earth.

For twenty years at the Cathedral of St. John the Divine we have been working to spread the *green* message—and for years many people thought we were a bit crazy. What is the connection between recycling and the Gospel?—Why do you have a blue crab in the Cathedral? Why do you bless animals on St. Francis Day? Now, at Rio, we saw the world, together at last, be exposed to, and for the most part, *get* the green message.

Cathedral Regent Maurice Strong, in *Green Cathedral,* a special issue of *Cathedral* put out for Rio, makes two points we must always keep in mind. The first concerns the common origin of two words: *ecology* and *economy*. *Ecology* is about the organizing and keeping of our household, Earth, how we've got to care for it and keep it clean; *economics* is about how you get the money and the food to all the folks in the house, the laws governing the flow of goods. Maurice Strong said that Rio makes clear to the whole world that the concern for *poverty and ecology must always go together.* We've got to have both.

The second point is that after Rio *there's no turning back.* Rio marks a turning point, and in the years ahead we will speak of the world's *change of mind* and its new hope, dating from the first UNCED, dating from Rio.

We are now brought full circle. We come again to that picture of our space island home. We have learned in these last twenty years that we are all stardust, we are all a bit of the detritus of an exploded star. We humans, dust, stardust, are part of the Earth, part of the mustard seed and part of the rainbow. With this realization comes the awareness that if we are to survive, we must meet the challenge to preserve, reclaim, and cherish Gaia our earthly home. This is the message for religious and secular leaders alike. Now, before it is too late, all humanity must come together to wipe out war and hunger and poverty and wanton destruction of life and nature; we must abandon our profligate, polluting ways. We must acknowledge the interdependence of the entire family of this living, breathing planet. We must keep before us the image of unity, of oneness in diversity, and all that means.

We must keep before us that new icon, that new rose window—that reverberating mandala, the music of the spheres—of all God's creation; and, hopefully, we will now learn to cherish this sacred orb, our holy home, the shimmering, blue-green planet . . . Earth.

✦ *16* ✦

Awakening to the World of God's Creation

by MICHAL FOX SMART

The ground is still wet as my partner and I survey our camp-site. Ten . . . eleven . . . yes, twelve students still sleeping peacefully, each snuggled in his or her sleeping bag with the drawstring pulled tight. Our tents have withstood the night's wind, the group food and gear have remained safe from unexpected animal visitors, and so, gratefully, we begin to plan the day ahead.

We are an unusual group: a dozen adolescents and three leaders, all Jews, who have decided to leave our urban homes for one month and to live as a Jewish community in the wilderness.[1] We read in Genesis that God commanded Abraham: "Get up, and walk in the land (of Canaan), to its length and width, because to you will I give it" (Genesis 13:17). Commentators explain the commandment: "So that he [Abraham] would come to grasp onto it [the land]." The biblical narrative implies that Abraham could not relate to the Promised Land in an abstract, intellectual fashion. Rather, he had to walk through the land; to climb its slopes and cross its streams, to feel its heat and find its shade, to encounter its flowers and fauna, to protect himself from its dangers, and in these ways to forge a covenant with it. And so we have come, not to address the environmental crisis through dispassionate discourse, but rather to rekindle our connection to the natural world and attempt to found an intimate relationship with a wild place. As the Bible suggests, this type

133

of intimate knowledge is necessary between people and the land, whose destinies are intertwined.

Our activities are varied: rock climbing, canoeing, backpacking through diverse environments, and a twenty-four hour solo by each person. In addition to the excitement they offer, these adventure activities engender personal growth in each participant as well as foster a tight-knit and interdependent community. They are common components of outdoor educational programs. As Jews, however, we are also here to reap the spiritual benefits of wilderness experience, to perceive and reflect on the life both around and within us in the world of God's creation. Throughout our journey, we strive to respect the life forms in the areas through which we travel, and to nurture spiritual growth through the unique framework of Jewish observance.

"Blessed are you, Lord our God . . . who shines upon the Earth and on those who dwell upon her in mercy, and who renews each day, always, the act of Creation." . . . Awakening each morning on a misty mountainside at daybreak, or in the desert as the early light begins to warm the weathered sandstone, the familiar words of our daily prayers come alive in a new way. The rainbows that span the canyon, the fragrance of the evening primrose, even the lightning storms that rip our tents and chase us off the mountain pass are acknowledged with traditional blessings that transform these experiences into a powerful introduction to Jewish spirituality and belief.

As our ancestors traversed the desert of Sinai with the Tabernacle in their midst, we, too, journey through the wilderness with a scroll of the Torah. We study the Torah in depth each Shabbat, and look to it for guidance in the building of our community and in our interaction with the land and other life forms. We ask what it means to walk through God's world as a Jew; where is the space for spirituality in our lives, and what is our role in the larger community of other peoples and species? In fact, the whole trip is framed as a rite of passage in which each participant receives the Torah anew and renews his or her covenant with God. This personal covenant, formed and defined throughout our journey, is bound up in the complex web of encounters and challenges that each person will experience in the wilderness.

And so, with hearts full with the richness of our surroundings and with the privilege of living, my partner and I excitedly awaken the participants. At the moment they're groaning at the lingering darkness and cold. Yet a day of discoveries awaits us.

＊　　＊　　＊

Sh' ma

Still for a moment
planted on the forest floor
I gaze at the berries
succulent and red
I allow the moss
which drapes the branch to my right
to caress my face
and I try to stand very still

As my thoughts resistantly quiet
I notice the droplets
leftovers
from this morning's rain
dangling from the tips of small leaves
like a crystal chandelier
that used to hang in my bubbe's apartment
When I crouch down to look through them
the world is a blur of color and light

Hands raised to my head
my ears mock those of my four-legged sister
and I listen:
I hear the crunch of friendly footsteps
I hear the flutelike voice
of a far-off bird
dancing in the unfamiliar space of silence

I hear the leaves, curled within their autumnal repose
crinkling in the breeze
sighing each time they exhale
and I feel that same breath enter my body
and exit again

God says to Israel: Sh' ma²
If you want to know me, listen
Pay attention
the next time a stranger tells you her name
Stroke the leaves of the nearest tree
if you strive to forge a covenant with me
Feel yourself a part of my breathing creation
My breath is in you; my life surrounds you
Sh'ma Yisrael
I am close at hand

+ *17* +

Planting Seeds of Joy

by STEPHANIE KAZA

On my altar at home stands a small bronze casting of Kuan Yin, the bodhisattva of compassion. Surrounded by redwood stems and acorns, she listens to the cries of the world with equanimity. On my desk is an image of the Buddha in meditation. He is touching the Earth with his right hand to counter the forces of ignorance. My third friend and teacher is Manjusri, the bodhisattva of wisdom, fierce protector of the truth. With his sharp sword he cuts through delusion, seeking insight into the nature of reality.

The courage and inspiration of the Buddha and bodhisattvas, or enlightened beings, are helpful to me in examining the spiritual dimension of the environmental crisis. They offer a model of radical presence in the world, of no separation between the one who suffers and the one who responds.[1] Like many others dedicated to environmental work, I move through waves of grief, rage, concern, and fear for the health of the planet. The extent of the damage is both debilitating and motivating. It seems certain that the scale of destruction has gone far beyond any ecological suffering known in the Buddha's time, yet I am confident that the Buddha's teachings are very relevant and useful for today's global crisis.

What is a Buddhist spiritual response to this serious state of affairs? What tools does this tradition offer that may be helpful in cultivating spiritual integrity and confidence to act? Which teachings of the Buddha can be applied to the complex environmental problems we face today? Concerned Buddhists in both the East and West are searching for answers to these questions. As in many traditions, we will need to apply Buddhist practice and philosophy in new ways to develop spiritually informed and environmentally sane modes of survival. I believe the self-disciplinary, analytic, and contemplative practices of Buddhism offer a powerful contribution to the urgent conversation of our times.

It may be no accident that the latest wave of Buddhist spiritual inquiry is most vital in North America, where environmental awareness and activism are most widespread.[2] The development of American Buddhism in the twentieth century will likely be influenced by citizen campaigns, green consumerism, and bioregional planning. Students of Buddhism with strong practice and clear intention may be of great service to the environmental movement— encouraging the greening of Buddhist practice centers, working in conflict mediation, or promoting interfaith dialogue.[3] Likewise, the environmental situation may serve the evolution of Buddhism by generating new expressions of a very old lineage of teaching.

In this essay, I look to fundamental Buddhist philosophy and practices for spiritual direction in meeting the challenges of today's ecological crisis. I begin with environmental suffering and the need to understand root causes. Then I consider how active spiritual attention to peace and love can create a basis for harmonious relations. I emphasize the importance of cultivating intimate relationships with the natural world and undertaking this work in the company of spiritual friends. It is my hope and desire that this writing will serve all beings in the struggle for existence.

Environmental Suffering

If one looks into the environmental situation, even superficially, the suffering of plants and animals, forests and rivers, local and indigenous peoples, is enormous. Wide-scale loss of habitat alone has caused countless deaths of individuals and extinction of an increasing number of species. In the Buddha's moment of profound awakening, he saw that all of life is mutually conditioned, that nothing exists as a separate or independent self. This truth, *paticca-samupadda,* or dependent co-arising, points to the commonality of impermanence shared by all forms of existence—from mayflies to mountains. Suffering naturally arises from impermanence, from constant change and loss. However, in the last century, the scale of suffering has accelerated significantly, to the point of threatening the continuity of life.

The Buddha's Four Noble Truths offer a path to understanding through the study of suffering. The first truth establishes the nature of existence as suffering. Birth, sickness, old age, and death—whether of house cats, grandparents, creeks, love affairs, or institutions—are all marked by suffering. In his precepts of the Order of Interbeing, Vietnamese Zen monk, Thich Nhat Hanh urges, "Do not avoid contact with suffering or close your eyes before suffering."[4] By opening to suffering, one gains a direct and moving experience of the nature of existence. To see a once-whole forest clearcut to stumps, the soil eroding, the wildlife gone, is to experience the impact of environmental suffering.

The second Noble Truth is that the cause of suffering is ignorance, which gives rise to greed, fear, anger, and other painful mental and emotional states. These states of mind cause people to objectify other beings into consumable goods. Through Buddhist spiritual practice one can examine the consequences of environmental ignorance and see in detail the causes and conditions that perpetuate damage to the Earth. This means becoming aware of physical and ecological ignorance and also of dualistic, objectifying habits of mind.

The Third Noble Truth is that there can be an end to suffering, that one can find liberation from the traps of conceiving of the self as a distinct and separate identity. In an ecological sense, this liberation must also be from the nationalistic or local delusions of environmental autonomy. In fact, the movement of air and water transcends political boundaries. Accepting the possibility of liberation, one cultivates a strong intention to overcome barriers of separation.

The path to freedom from delusion lies in the Fourth Noble Truth—the Buddha's prescription for realization of the impermanent and interdependent nature of reality. This is the Eightfold Path of Right Understanding, Right Mindfulness, Right Speech, Right Action, Right Livelihood, Right Effort, Right Attention, and Right Concentration. Each of these spokes of the wheel offers one arena in which spiritual practice can bring awareness to the environmental crisis.

The four Noble Truths can be applied as a framework for spiritual inquiry into specific environmental situations by posing four questions: (1) What is the problem or the suffering? (2) What are the causes of the suffering? (3) What would put an end to the suffering? (4) What is the path to realize this goal?[5] This analysis is deceptively simple, yet it is radical in including all forms of suffering—from individual people, animals, and trees to populations, communities, and ecosystems. It is also radical in that it cultivates compassion by directing attention to the actual suffering, thereby evoking a response of kindness and desire to alleviate suffering. I find this a refreshing alternative to technological or politically driven approaches that de-emphasize expression of concern or heartfelt relationship with those who are suffering.

Investigative spiritual practice can be very important in breaking through the mental habits of denial and idealization. When people understate or overstate environmental problems they compound the suffering, obscuring the way to acceptable solutions. A person in denial of global warming, habitat loss, or nuclear contamination—whether from fear, helplessness, or political pressure—blocks effective problem solving. Drugs and television that distance people from the natural world perpetuate an illusion of safety and isolation. Likewise, consumerism, in camouflaging the suffering behind produced goods encourages false relief from moral responsibility. Factory-farmed chickens, for example, are raised in extremely restrictive cages and processed at a pace that causes crippling diseases in very young women.[6] Vegetables grown on large-scale agribusiness farms require pesticide poisoning of the soil.[7]

In contrast, the person who romanticizes nature favors an idealized view, often based in nostalgia. The idealized view obscures the actual reality that may be hard to accept. In the tourist state of Vermont, known for its fall foliage and skiing, many locals ignore severe air pollution in late summer because they are economically dependent on the state's image. In a similar way, those who idealize native peoples and their spiritual traditions may overlook serious health threats for tribes living near nuclear waste dumps.

Buddhist mindfulness practice can be used in observing emotional and mental responses to environmental suffering. For the concerned and compassionate person, emotional impacts come with the territory of environmental work. When I was teaching a course in International Environmental Studies to 230 undergraduates, I frequently found myself distraught after a lecture, overwhelmed by the dimensions of rain-forest destruction, desertification, or human rights abuses associated with environmental plunder. Drawing on the practices of meditation and compassion, I struggled to be present with the reality of environmental damage while maintaining a steady intention.

Through training with Joanna Macy, activist and spiritual teacher, I have come to accept the emotions themselves as indicators of the unsatisfactory moral quality of existing environmental relationships. Macy uses Buddhist meditation practices to go to the heart of personal response to the environmental crisis.[8] Her work is echoed by feminist theologian Bev Harrison who suggests that anger can be seen as a "feeling-signal that all is not well in our relation to others or to the world around us."[9] She argues that the power to respond to feeling is the power to create a world of moral relations. The spiritual practitioner who cultivates mindfulness in emotional response to suffering can bring compassion and understanding to those engaged in political battles for the environment.

Seeds of Joy

Awareness of environmental suffering by itself is not enough to generate a positive vision for the future. To nourish actively the storehouse of consciousness, Thich Nhat Hanh advocates being in touch with "what is wondrous, refreshing, and healing both inside yourself and around yourself."[10] His *gathas,* or meditation poems, cultivate spiritual attitudes that refresh the mind:

> Breathing in, I calm my body.
> Breathing out, I smile.
> Dwelling in the present moment,
> I know this is a wonderful moment!
>
> Water flows from high in the mountains.
> Water runs deep in the earth.

Miraculously, water comes to us
and sustains all life.[11]

He urges maintaining a half smile to stimulate positive energy, even under difficult conditions.

By planting seeds of joy, peace, and understanding in one's self, one facilitates the work of transformation in the inner consciousness. Reactions of anger and frustration, for example, in dealing with recalcitrant corporate polluters or uncooperative government officials, can be greatly mitigated by cultivating experiences of deep joy. The joy itself softens and outlasts the anger, reinforcing a sincere desire for the happiness of all beings. Joy may come from outdoor sensory contact with the natural world or quiet meditative practices that renew a sense of connection. By cultivating an internal reference point of joy, independent of shifting external circumstances, a spiritually trained environmentalist prepares to work for the long haul. This strength of intention can inspire others to steadiness in their efforts.

Joy and peace develop most easily through love. The Buddha emphasized two kinds of love: *karuna*, or compassion, and *metta*, or loving kindness. *Karuna* arises as the natural and spontaneous response of the heart to the suffering of others, often felt as the desire to help alleviate their pain. The capacity for compassion grows through opening the heart to circumstances filled with difficulty. This kind of spiritual effort can be extremely challenging in the face of massive forest destruction or slaughter of endangered species for trade. But to turn away from the pain is to close the heart, and therefore the mind, to the complexity and suffering of the ecological web.

Metta, or loving kindness, may be practiced independently of specific situations of suffering. The cultivation of metta is a matter of prayer, offering well-wishing on behalf of one's self, one's friends and family, even one's enemies, and then all beings. Cambodian monk Maha Ghosananda offers this prayer as an expression of metta in the Theravadin tradition of Southeast Asia:

May all beings exist in happiness and peace.
The suffering of Cambodia has been deep.

> From this suffering comes great compassion.
> Great compassion makes a peaceful heart.
> A peaceful heart makes a peaceful person.
> A peaceful person makes a peaceful family.
> A peaceful family makes a peaceful community.
> A peaceful community makes a peaceful nation.
> A peaceful nation makes a peaceful world.[12]

To say such prayers on a regular basis develops the habit of thinking positively of others, whether plants, animals, or people. The internal mantra of well-wishing becomes more than a nice idea; it can be an actual force of renewal in the universe, affecting a person's environmental negotiations and creative problem solving. Words of loving kindness can encourage others to experience the love and beauty of the Earth, thus planting seeds of joy that may motivate and support a life of ecological sanity and sustainability.

For His Holiness, the Dalai Lama of Tibet, kindness is the heart of Buddhist practice and human relations. He advocates following a "policy of kindness"[13] no matter how troublesome the situation, preferring this approach to the lofty declaration of institutional doctrines or ideals. This might be called Buddhism with a small *b*, the everyday invisible challenge of simply getting along with the environment and each other.[14] As an example of this policy of kindness, the Dalai Lama has proposed that Tibet be declared a zone of *Ahimsa*, or nonharming, i.e., a nationwide ecological reserve.[15] Though Tibetans support this idea, Ahimsa is not possible because of Chinese suppression of human rights and escalation of environmental plundering.

A policy of kindness toward trees, rivers, air, and mountains implies careful attention to each relationship that makes up the interdependent web of life. This policy extended equally to human beings would smooth the way toward resolution of polarized, dualistic battles pitting forests against loggers, medicinal plants against indigenous tribes, dolphins against fishermen. A Buddhist approach to environmental conflict resolution is fundamentally based on metta and karuna. When people are motivated by a genuine desire for harmonious relations, they bring a creative openness and refreshing willingness to the problem at hand. One person's capacity to refrain from defensive postures can allow a breakthrough in communication for a whole group. In combination with the compassionate force of Buddhist analysis, the practice of metta can generate fo˙ ward movement in the midst of great crisis. As His Holiness points out,

> When we talk about preservation of the environment, it is re-
> lated to many other things. Ultimately, the decision must come
> from the human heart. The key point is to have a genuine sense
> of universal responsibility, based on love and compassion, and
> clear awareness.[16]

Cultivating Intimacy

Of all the Buddha's teachings, one of the most central is that each person must find the Way of Truth for him or herself. The Buddha claimed no ultimate, absolute source of wisdom and enlightenment and offered no easy answers to those who engage in spiritual inquiry. He insisted that each person must study reality in depth, understanding suffering and dependent co-arising in the context of his or her own life. In the Buddhist texts, true knowledge is not seen as any final doctrinal truth, but as deep awareness of the process of knowing itself.

Direct knowing frees the mind to grasp fully and immediately the truth of the environmental web of relationships that support human life. Practices that quiet and focus the mind allow a person to cultivate intimate familiarity with the subtle aspects of consciousness. Opening to the true nature of existence, one may experience an intimate and awesome sense of connection with all beings. As one enters fully into the web, one gains a legitimate voice to speak of environmental relationships that have been ignored or damaged. Torn by the accelerating loss of temperate and tropical forests, I have felt compelled to speak out on behalf of trees. I have gone directly to the trees of my region to ask for counsel and stories.[17] It has taken time to learn to listen deeply in each encounter. I have attempted simply to be present with the trees, allowing them to guide my spiritual training and political responses. Each meeting has deepened my desire for intimacy with nonhuman beings and increased my confidence in the joy of relationship.

This work has not been without difficulty, however. As a Westerner, I have inherited the cultural conditioning of seeing plants and animals as separate objects or resources. The habit of objectivity easily overrules and silences the voice of intimacy. To reawaken spiritual connections with the environment requires deconditioning the objectifying mind. Through the Buddhist practice of discriminating awareness, one can see through concepts such as "board feet of timber," "game management," and "economic development." One's spiritual goal is to penetrate the objectifying mind to meet another being genuinely. This means going beyond generic archetypes to the unique history, geography, and relationships of each individual plant, animal, or ecosystem. The yearning for spiritual intimacy and interaction cannot be satisfied by generalized, oversimplified impressions.

Anthropocentric bias, central to Western ideology and economics, is perhaps one of the greatest deterrents to intimacy. If one sees the environment as primarily for human use—whether for food, shelter, recreation, or spiritual development—it is difficult to perceive the intrinsic nature of another being. Observing and correcting Western anthropocentric habits in all their complex and varied guises offers a lifetime of spiritual work. The Buddhist discipline of rigorous observation of the body-mind is very helpful in undertaking this challenging process of deconditioning.

I see this work as spiritual practice because it goes to the core of the ego-generating habit of mind. A primary effort in Buddhist training is to see how the mind constructs the illusion of a separate self. I believe the parallel environmental work is to investigate the cultural concepts that perpetuate the illusion of society as separate from the larger interdependent web of the natural world. This is not easy work; it is not a matter of false ideas being embedded only in someone else's mind. To acknowledge them in one's own mind is to face full complicity with the destructive effects of jet planes, automobiles, imported food, shopping malls, and copy machines. With some humility, one accepts the difficult struggle of simply seeing what we are doing.

Waking up Together

Liberty Hyde Bailey, an American naturalist at the turn of the century, said, "The happiest life has the greatest number of points of contact with the world, and it has the deepest feeling and sympathy with everything that is."[18] I interpret this to mean that the joy of relating with others is the source of spiritual happiness. By this I do not refer to the generic experience of "at-one-ness" or cosmic unity with the natural world. I mean the actual day-to-day participation in specific relationships with specific nonhuman and human beings. This is what I call the cultivation of *relational richness*. One may engage in relationship with the moon, observing its waxing and waning cycle, position in the sky, and effect on one's moods and energy. One may cultivate relationships with migrating shorebirds, hatching dragonflies, or ancient redwoods. One may learn the topography of local rivers and mountains. These relations are not onetime encounters; rather they are ongoing friendships. Over time, they grow richer and come to define the terrain of one's existence. The greater the number of these points of contact and the longer the history of engagement with each one, the richer the experience of participating in the interdependent web.

Unfortunately, the opportunities for relational richness have been severely curtailed in many places because of ecological damage. Water pollution, loss of forests, and pesticide contamination have reduced local populations, limiting the chances for even first-time meetings. In these cases, ecological restoration becomes a practice of spiritual restoration, motivated by the desire for a relationally rich life. On Arbor Day at Green Gulch Farm and Zen Center in California, our tree planting is a joyful invitation for birds, wildflowers, and deer to return to the area. In this request lies the need and desire for spiritual community, the yearning for friendships not only with people, but also with animals, plants, land, and water.

Central to Buddhist practice is taking refuge in the Three Treasures—the *Buddha*, the *Dharma*, and the *Sangha*. In vowing not to abuse the Three Treasures, one acknowledges internal reference points for acting in the world. The Buddha is the teacher or source of teachings manifesting in many different awakened forms. The great horned owl Buddha offers teachings on stillness and the dark night; the creek Buddha speaks the teachings of water. Gophers, redwoods, and prominent peaks all carry their own evolutionary truth that informs and enriches our lives.

The Dharma is the truth of relationship and interdependence.

Each step, each moment, each place is a manifestation of co-conditioned relationship, shaped by the landscape as well as the mind of the one who walks in the landscape. Each experience of connection with members of the environmental web is a taste of the deeply intimate and intersupportive nature of reality.

Sangha has traditionally meant the monastic community or those who practice in a specific group or setting. As Buddhism matures in the West, the definition of sangha is evolving to include nonmonastics and for some, the plants and animals of the local environmental web. The largest sense of community is all beings practicing together, sharing a commonality of impermanence. Deep ecologist Bill Devall describes this as the *ecocentric sangha,* in which spiritual practice is a practice of place, where one is located in community and responding to a wider web of relationships.[19] One then sits in meditation not only with people but also with the surrounding oaks, maples, jays, warblers, and lupines.

Under the pressures of modern life, one of the most difficult tasks is to slow down enough simply to "be present." To listen to the teachings of owl Buddha or pill-bug Buddha requires time not dedicated to other tasks. The time-proven spiritual practices of restraint, moderation, and simplicity increase the odds for more time in relationship, more time for waking up together. The ecological need to reduce consumption of material goods can be a spiritual practice, based in the desire for more genuine contact with others. The desire to reduce clutter and possessions can be the desire to live actively in relationship rather than protected from it. Reducing time spent in dealing with objects (cars, videos, furniture, toys) allows time for actively cultivating intimacy with rivers and mountains, moon, and stars. Television alone may rob American culture of many hours that could be spent fostering relationships with real animals and real trees rather than cartoons and advertisements. Zen teacher Robert Aitken suggests a vow of simplicity:

> Hearing the crickets at night
> I vow with all beings
> to keep my practice simple—
> just over and over again.[20]

One of the Buddha's students once remarked that it seemed to him that having good friends was half of the holy life. "Not so," the Buddha replied. "Having good friends is the whole of spiritual life." *Kalyana mitta,* or spiritual friends, can help each other by offering compassion in the face of tragic environmental suffering and by working together to restore environmentally damaged areas. Dharma friends can investigate rigorously the mental blocks to relational intimacy. They can share delight and offer gratitude for the Earth as home. American Buddhists have tended to place primary dependence on relationships with spiritual teachers, reinforcing a hierarchical view of authority. I am coming to see that shifting the balance of learning toward spiritual friendships is critical for environmental work. Hindu teacher Dr. Raymundo Panikkar suggests that the real work of the future is not to build great temples of religion in search of understanding, but "to simply follow the well-worn paths between one another's houses."[21]

As spiritual friends in a complex, ecological world, we can help each other wake up to the splendid, if troubled, multidimensional reality of the environment. I believe it is our spiritual task to help each other bear the generational responsibility for turning the tide of ecological destruction. In the company of spiritual friends, we can learn to be present with the physical, mental, emotional, and spiritual suffering of environmental loss. We can help each other maintain our courage and motivation to act boldly. Together we can plant the seeds of joy that will nurture sustainable spiritual relations with all beings far into the future.

✦ *18* ✦

Dwelling

by WM. JAMES RILEY

Each of us
   is responsible
      to those who dwelled here before us
      and those who will inherit our decisions.
What we do now
   will be recorded
      not only in the mind of God
      but in the bowels of the Earth
      where trees invent their roots.
The Earth is alive
   with the ecstasy of those
      who dwell forever in a place
      our spirit knows as home.
Home is the membrane
   that envelopes spirit in a face and character
      for only within limits is the infinite real
      and only within boundaries is the Earth whole.
Boundary marks the gateway between here and there
   without which place is only space ungrounded
      and one space the same as any other.
In a world without places
   there is no responsibility for yesterday and tomorrow.

◆ *19* ◆

Practical Environmental Mythology

by JOSEPH W. MEEKER

Not long ago I was in Mesa Verde National Park, one of the world's magical places. I was exploring kivas, the ceremonial caves in the Earth where the Anasazi went for spiritual renewal. In a kiva, the shaman always occupied the lowest place, closest to the Earth. The Western tradition, by contrast, thinks of leadership coming from up above, where the priests and gods are. Structures reflect the mythic beliefs of those who build them. The way people design the spaces where we come together to learn and think is one of the clearest manifestations of practical environmental mythology.

The cliff dwellings of Mesa Verde, occupied between about A.D. 700 and 1200, represent the spiritual vision and the practical good sense of the people who built them. The dwellings are nestled into eroded parts of the mountainside. The structures in those spaces are made of the same materials as the cliffs, a beautiful tan sandstone, and the architecture is such that it is almost impossible to tell where the geology ends and the buildings begin. There is a seamless transition from nonhuman rock to human habitation. Visiting a place like that makes you wonder what it would feel like to have a philosophy that was fully embedded and embodied in your dwelling. I can imagine that the life the people lived in that space was the same. Their lives must have been part of the environment, not at war with it, or in defense against it, or in aggrandizement of it, but a simple continuity as the events of human life flowed from the natural setting. Their architecture and their mythology were one.

The mythology that guides our perceptions of who and where we are is not just found in the ancient stories that we have inherited from the past. We are continually involved in making and revising our own myths. I saw an example of that during the 1989 Loma Prieta earthquake, in which I was privileged to participate (I am a connossieur of earthquakes and volcanoes). The Earth spoke clearly that day in the Bay Area. After the quake, I listened as people told their stories, for virtually everyone had a story to tell. You could walk up to anyone in the Bay Area and ask, "Where were you during the quake?" and you would hear the story of where they were, what happened, how they reacted. A year or more later, the same people tell the same stories, but their literary quality has improved. The stories have been transformed: they have been edited, they've become more interesting, they are better focused, their language is enriched. At first, people didn't know quite how to tell their stories, but later the stories became works of art. As I listened to scores of quake stories, I began to notice that they don't tell very much about the earthquake, but they do say a lot about the person who is telling the story. Some stories are heroic, some are adventurous, some are comic, some speak of divine retribution or punishment, or of divine intervention, or of helplessness in the face of great powers. These are the themes upon which the great myths are based, elicited in our time by a 7.3 tremor.

That earthquake did more to raise environmental consciousness than all the preachings of conservation groups. Here was no invisible ozone problem or decimation of unseen tropical forests, but the very ground beneath our feet transformed into liquid, crushing the symbols of human mastery (freeways, bridges, buildings) as if they were of no importance. The normal human response to such events is to tell stories, and the stories eventually become the myths that redefine our relationship to the Earth. People of the Pacific Northwest did the same a decade ago at the last eruption of Mt. St. Helens. When the Earth speaks to us with strength, we answer with creative mythology.

We participate in creating the mythology of our time. We're lucky to have some wonderful materials to work into our stories that other people have not known about. We can now tell our earthquake and volcano stories with the help of geologists who inform us about the movements of tectonic plates and give us some sense of how our earthquakes fit into the ancient history of the planet. Science provides us with elaborate story materials from physics, chemistry, astronomy, geology, ecology, and evolutionary history that can enrich every story we tell.

Stories are most often told in a conversational setting, through the personal relationships we share with one another. I think that conversation itself is a mythic activity. Conversation is quite unlike the other kinds of discourse in which we participate. It is not like preaching, or selling, or seducing, or lecturing, or arguing, or persuading. There is something special about ordinary conversation, when you meet your neighbor in a checkout line, and exchange information: How are the kids? How are you feeling? What are you doing these days? How's that arthritis? You look worried—what's on your mind? How can I help? That kind of conversation, exchanging information about what's going on in our lives, is a form of art that is not taught in the schools, that we do not, fortunately, learn from any authority. No one can teach us how to converse, for it is an art that has emerged for each of us from our biological history.

The way in which we engage in ordinary conversation with one another has probably not changed much since the early Paleolithic Age, some fifty thousand years ago. A conversation in the checkout line is much the same as the conversation we might have had if we were skinning a wildebeest together in 20,000 BC, the Paleolithic equivalent of the supermarket. What people talk about while they prepare food has probably not changed much over the millenia. Our other forms of discourse are subject to dramatic shifts and changes in style. Scientific language changes rapidly; we discuss religion according to the habits of various sects and traditions; politics invents a new language for every change in power; debating styles are transformed from generation to generation. The languages of institutional and public discourse are fashionable affairs, following the fads of the moment. But personal conversation remains remarkably constant: we could recognize patterns of conversation among ancient Romans, Hindu ascetics, or Kalahari Bushmen to be very like our own. The reason is that conversation is rooted not in our cultures, but in our biology as human beings.

Some recent research has documented how our bodies respond when we are engaged in conversation. Dr. James Lynch, in a book called *The Language of the Heart* shows how conversation is accompanied by dramatic changes in blood pressure, skin temperature, heart rate, and many other physiological variables, even including exchange of blood gases. People who are involved in these conversations are generally unaware of the important changes taking place within their bodies as they engage in ordinary chitchat with a friend, or even with a familiar animal like a dog or cat. Our bodies are involved in biological exchanges when we talk with one another, and these may be every bit as significant as the verbal information we share. It may be that the words we use are small parts of the large exchanges that take place during conversation, not the main show that we take them to be. When we talk together, we are in a mutual exchange of biological subtleties that far outweighs the lexical information we pass back and forth. We converse out of our evolutionary history as mammals.

We respond to one another as *whole people*, not just as carriers of verbal information. When we tell our stories, and listen to the stories of others, every part of us is involved in the process. One reason we may not be aware of all this is that we are educated. Education tells us what we should perceive and pay attention to: this is success, this is failure, this is significant, this is trivial. We learn our culture's ideas about what is important to notice, and how to react to the world, but we don't learn to pay much heed to the states of our own bodies, or to the subtle processes of our interactions. Whether we are aware of it or not, our bodily systems of perception and communication are working all the time, just as they have been for hundreds of thousands of years. Those ancient systems may be buried under layers of language and culture, but they remain a part of us, and they are accessible to us if we seek them.

Learning to listen to our bodies is the beginning of practical, applied mythology. We can attend to the earthquakes and volcanoes within ourselves as our blood pressure, temperature, and our feelings send us their clear messages. The messages come not only from our present circumstances, but also from our evolutionary history, and from the origins of life. We are carriers of all that has gone before us. There are stories being told within us that we scarcely know how to hear.

We need to be in conversation with our own bodies, with one another, and with the natural world from which our perceptions have grown. We can talk with plants and animals, and if we listen carefully, we will get answers from them. Conversation works well across species lines with any part of the world around us, and that can become another source for practical environmental mythology. The things that interest us in conversation with other people are the same things we need to know about other species: How are you doing? How do you make your living? How are your relatives? How is your health? Are you in danger? Is there any way I can help you? For those kinds of questions, every creature around us has an answer. They all have relatives, all earn their daily seeds and meat, all depend upon their context for health and well-being, and they all participate in the daily business of living in the same sense that we do. The information that people share in conversation is the same information we need from the other creatures around us.

I have a story. It's about Bodie, an eight-year-old boy who has been living in my house for the past year. Bodie has been unhappily separated from his parents, and this has been a year of recovery for him. Bodie came home from school one day feeling very angry. Maybe he had been humiliated, or hurt, or any of the thousand awful things that can happen in the course of a school day. He didn't want to talk about it, but he went to his toolbox and got his hammer, then went outside. I followed at a distance, and saw him go to a large rock near the entrance to our driveway. He raised the hammer and started beating the rock mercilessly, sending chunks of granite flying, intent upon punishing it. I yelled to him to stop, then explained that the rock was a friend of mine. I told him what I knew of the rock's history, how granite is formed, and how the rock had been deposited there by the Vashon glaciation some thirteen thousand years ago. I also told him about the time I had tried to move this eight-hundred-pound boulder, and had been defeated by it. Then I said that I thought Bodie owed the rock an apology for what he had done to it. He looked at me as if I were a little crazy, didn't say anything, and went off to do something else. Our conversation ended.

A few days later, Bodie came home from school in a pensive mood. It was a rainy day, and after his snack, he put on his raincoat and went outside. He walked down the driveway and sat on the same rock that he had attacked. When I came within earshot, I could hear that Bodie was talking to the rock. He told it what he had done during the day and how he was feeling. He spent perhaps ten minutes in conversation with the rock, then went next door to play with the neighbor kids. Over the following week, Bodie returned to the rock several times.

Bodie knows what it means to feel the weight of someone else's power, and to be defenseless against it. He knows what abuse means. Perhaps he had some empathy with that rock. Whatever happened, I think Bodie was in a two-way conversation with the rock, receiving something from it while he was giving to it. He was in a healing conversation, for himself and for the rock.

Maybe we're all a little like Bodie, aware that we've been beating on this rock we call the Earth for a long time, and wanting to find a healthier relationship with it. One way to make amends, to restore relationship, to heal ourselves, is to enter into some kind of conversation with the abused Earth. We have a role to play in the Earth's story, and we can renew our conversation with the Earth in order to explore the story we share with it. Conversation is not about information, but about relationships. Good conversation is a ritual affirmation of the web of relationships that can make life whole. It leads toward a practical environmental mythology that we can live with every day. Like the Anasazi, we too are capable of creating spaces that fit the land we live upon, and we have the power to tell stories that affirm ourselves while celebrating the Earth.

✦ 20 ✦

Action, Absurdity, and Faith

by ALAN AtKISSON

Will it be possible to heal the Earth? Will it be possible to heal even one small piece of it, when our lives are embedded in systems that force us into behaviors that do the Earth harm, even as we work to heal?

Upon leaving the environmental conference, committee meeting, or church service—hearts full, action agendas in hand—we get into our planes and our cars and make our daily contribution to global warming, air pollution, the poisoning of water, the extinction of wildlife, the impoverishment of our own children. We send messages on virgin paper to grieve the loss of trees. Even those who strive to avoid these collusions—who go by bicycle or by foot, who eat organic vegetables, who recycle everything—will inevitably find themselves under an electric light bulb powered by splitting atoms or fossil fuels.

If aware of the irony, we often respond in one of two ways: with irony itself, with its detached and sardonic smile; or with an uncomfortable sense of hypocrisy that neatly undermines our recently made commitments. In the first case, we are disempowered by cynicism. In the second, by shame. And the transformation that threatens to slip behind the horizon, eclipsed by the absurdity of the world we and our ancestors have labored hard and well to build.

It is nothing but faith, of course, that gives our actions and our commitments meaning in the face of life's inevitable craziness. Faith that every action we take, no matter how small, matters. Faith that the genius of Creation is not daunted by what appears to us as a future of labyrinthine complexity and danger.

But this faith is much more than mere belief that all will be well, that meaning will win out in the end. I looked up the word *faith* in the dictionary recently and was reminded of its root in the Latin word *fidere*—to trust. Then a little note said, "more at *bide.*" *Bide* is an old word that lives on in our language in the phrase "to bide one's time," usually implying boredom. But in the past, to bide meant *to await confidently and defiantly.* The synonym offered was *withstand.*

This is what faith means, at its most nitty-gritty level. As we act to heal our hurting world—as we pledge ourselves to the task of converting meaninglessness into meaning, ignorance into intelligence, suffering into joy—there is much absurdity that we must abide, that we must withstand, with confidence and defiance in the face of very long odds.

We must, for example, abide the absurdity of knowing that the same human-created systems that support us, ennoble us, and give us pleasure are also destroying things that are precious to us. We must abide the absurdity of watching that destruction continue, carried by momentum, even after we begin to make transformative changes in those systems and in our lives.

We must also abide the feelings of guilt and shame at our inevitable complicity in destruction, and resist the temptation to disconnect from the modern world, even when that means continuing to participate in activities, like the inevitable act of driving, that we know to cause harm. Only if we stay engaged with the world as it is can we lend our weight to the transformative movements that will create a world that is sustainable.

Perhaps our greatest challenge is to withstand the burden of *awareness*—knowing what we know about the state of our beloved planet. Dying species, threats to forest and ocean and atmosphere, an intimacy with this suffering, and the grief that accompanies it, can and must be abided as a part of our faith.

And we must *continue* to act. The true test of faith is continuing to do something, even when that something seems fruitless. As Václav Havel said about hope, faith's fraternal twin: "Hope is . . .

not the conviction that something will turn out well, but the conviction that something makes sense, regardless of how it turns out."

A Western journalist in Tibet reported that he found a Tibetan lama, the last living monk in a monastery all but destroyed by the Chinese army. He was continuing to serve the frightened people of his village. The journalist asked him, "Why do you continue this work, when it is certain that the monastery will be destroyed, that you will be killed?" The monk looked at him with tenderness. "I do it to reduce the suffering," he said. Such is the expression of faith at its apogee.

It is my faith that we must keep a bright vision in front of our eyes, and dream of an Earth whose people are at peace with each other and the whole of life we call "nature." But let us not turn away from the truer, harsher tests that our vision must also withstand. Let us cultivate the strength of spirit always to act in faithfulness—and to abide.

✦ *21* ✦

Food as Sacrament

by MIRIAM THERESE MACGILLIS

> To live we must daily break the body and shed the blood
> of creation. When we do this knowingly, lovingly, skill-
> fully, reverently, it is a sacrament. When we do it igno-
> rantly, greedily, clumsily, destructively, it is a desecration.
> In such desecration we condemn ourselves to spiritual and
> moral loneliness and others to want.
>
> —*Wendell Berry*

In 1972 I laid down my paintbrushes. I packed away the fresh, barely opened prospects of life devoted to exploring my path as an artist and teacher, and set out on a strange, unanticipated journey for which I was neither ready nor prepared.

A student's questions had blown me away. She had been brooding like some wise old crone over the tragedy of war. It was 1967. She was seventeen. To her, Vietnam was an inscrutable mirror of all that was distorted in the American soul. She pinned me against the wall until I could finally admit to all the defenses of my entire life. She exposed my masks of virtue: selflessness, patriotism, trustfulness, obedience, humility, naïveté.

Five years after my dialogues with this young seer, I began my life all over again. I reentered kindergarten, you might say, and realized my only chance for living my life was to remain there. To leave, I would have to paint my tired old images of the world again. What made that decision most painful was that so many of the people I loved and respected had believed in my promise as a painter.

In the fall of 1972 I began an internship at the Institute of Justice and Peace, an educational program of the Roman Catholic Archdiocese of Newark, New Jersey. The diocese had a strong commitment to the rights of laborers and to the promotion of the social teachings of the Church. During the sixties, the city of Newark had exploded in racial riots and the Church had evolved as a strong voice for social and economic change. Now the issues of war and the ambiguity surrounding Vietnam were finding their place in the agenda of this small educational program.

Just about the time that I began my internship, the world was shaken by the impact of the Mideast oil embargo. The vibrations from the economic decisions of the oil cartel affected everyone, everywhere. In its wake, just as I was wrestling with the agenda of war and militarism, the specters of world hunger and famine arose as a vast backdrop against which all the perennial questions about violence, greed, racism, and dominance were played. The escalation of oil prices had set off the escalation of food prices and when the tremors of both those explosions subsided the way of life on our planet was altered irreparably.

My personal journey through the seventies was difficult. My naïveté about the world was shattered. How could it be that my species could be so offtrack in its direction? How did we come to have such misplaced priorities? How could I have been so asleep? How could it be that my culture was so asleep? My church? My Dominican congregation?

World hunger became a doorway for me. As I would probe one dimension of it, my studies would lead me to new doors, and these doors led to further doors. The interconnectedness of all the dimensions became apparent as I realized that the causes and effects were complex beyond my simple analysis. The devastation it wrought kept escalating. The suffering of millions of starving people was a daily reality. So was the bitter realization that there were no easy answers.

There were three strong lights on my journey to learn, understand, and keep going during these years. One was the social teaching of the Catholic church. Although I could not always see its effects in the pastoral life of local churches, I held firmly to the long, clear development of a consistent ethic for life that had emerged through the Church's social teachings. A century ago,

Pope Leo XIII had spoken clearly on the rights of workers and the ethics of labor. Through the early teachings of this century, into the era of the Second Vatican Council, the renewal of the Church became identified with the deepest human aspirations for a world of peace, self-empowerment, and justice in human structures.

The second light was the profound effect of meeting and working with Patricia and Gerald Mishe. They had founded Global Education Associates in 1973. Through their own lives of commitment, they had struggled to understand and analyze the same deep questions about the misplaced priorities and values of our contemporary world. Their depth of analysis was an enormous gift to me, and they gently led me into seeing historically and structurally. Their major contribution, *Toward a Human World Order: Beyond the National Security Straight-Jacket,* provided an invaluable framework for understanding the dilemmas inherent in the nation-state system as it grappled with the realities of a single interdependent planet. I began to understand that the values of a true and just world order could not be realized through the perceptions and values of a planet organized around separate national agendas.

In 1977 a third major light came to me through the work of Thomas Berry. His reflections on world order helped me to break through the limitations of anthropomorphism, a worldview that had shaped my entire consciousness. His interpretation of the New Cosmology literally opened the universe to me and profoundly influenced the direction of my work.

In 1980 I came to live and work at Genesis Farm, a 140-acre farm bequeathed to my Dominican congregation in 1978. It was founded on a vision of creating a space where people of goodwill could come to ask the critical questions around our contemporary crises. It was to be a reflection center where we would also grapple with the challenges of our Western life-style, our alienation from the natural world, and the issues of land, agriculture, and food.

Genesis Farm is a "learning center for re-inhabiting the Earth," a descriptive phrase taken from the writings of Thomas Berry. The two primary dimensions of our work are in the areas of *learning* and *agriculture*.

The *learnings* lead us to alter radically our perceptions of the origin and nature of the universe as a bio-spiritual reality. We work to heal the separation of matter and spirit, as that single human perception that has so intrinsically affected the beliefs upon which the whole of Western culture is founded. Our programs and workshops are designed to help us experience ourselves as a dimension *of* the Earth, and to expand our concept of *self* to include our *Earth self*, our *universe self*, as one single reality. This is no small undertaking. Redefining ourselves in a bioregional context has become a primary source of personal transformation. This, too, is profoundly challenging. Each of our programs takes these learnings as its starting point.

The second major thrust of Genesis Farm is in the area of what we now call "sacred agriculture." In the words of Vincent McNabb, O. P.:

> If there is one truth more than any other, which life and thought have made us admit, against our prejudices, and even against our will, it is that there is little hope of saving civilization or religion except by the return of contemplatives to the land.[1]

Laying a contemplative foundation for our work in sacred agriculture rests on two central bodies of thought that we try to integrate.

The first is the exploration of the Earth as a self-nourishing organism. This concept displaces the prevalent cultural assumption about the role of farmers as the "growers" of food. When we begin to grapple with the differences in these perceptions, it becomes obvious how enormous is the shift of consciousness demanded to transform agriculture as practiced in the industrialized world. There are scientific, educational, and economic institutions that would virtually collapse if this understanding became evident and operable in our human communities.

If we understood the Earth as a *living being* whose activities are to *nourish, govern, learn, heal, regenerate, and transform itself,* then the mystery at the heart of human existence would open up and draw us into the sacramental aspect of our lives through the most ordinary and familiar ways.

The second major influence in our farming comes from the philosophy of Rudolf Steiner, a practice known as biodynamic agriculture. Steiner lived in Austria at the turn of the century, and while he did not have available the insight drawn from quantum physics, or from the Gaia theory, or the observations of our space explorers, his knowledge of the spiritual world pervading the world of matter resulted in an approach to farming and to the nourishing function of food that is extraordinary. Since 1987 the fields and gardens of Genesis Farm have been cultivated with this biodynamic approach. The food from this garden is literally a manifestation of Spirit.

It has become clear to me that the concept of food itself is key to the transformation of our ecological crisis. Unless our human species can open itself to the contemplation of food as a holy mystery through which we *eat ourselves into existence*, then the meaning of existence will continue to elude us. Our present cultural experience of food has degenerated into food as *fuel*, for supplying the energy for our insatiable search for that which will fill the hungers of our soul. When we understand that food is not a metaphor for spiritual nourishment, but is itself spiritual, then we eat food with a spiritual attitude and taste and are nourished by the Divine *directly*.

From early times Western culture has carried the burden of guilt for the existence of chaos in the universe. Only now are we realizing that the universe was divinely organized from the beginning with chaos as an integral dimension. Our earlier perceptions have cast a shadow over the attitude with which Western peoples have "discovered" and evolved "agriculture." Feeling doomed to earn our bread by the sweat of our brow explains part of the deep, hidden rage against the natural world described by Thomas Berry.[2] Our propensity toward favoritism has closed us off to the full diversity of nourishment offered by the Earth. It has constrained us by the narrow choices we elected in our methodology of monoculture. This clearly has shaped our present agricultural crisis.

The determination to redeem the Earth and transcend its natural limitations has played itself out in the industrialization and total mechanization of farming. The soils have been exhausted and drugged, their inner life forces depleted and poisoned, not because we are necessarily an evil species so much as that we are driven by our abstract *ideas* about a perfect world. We have been inculturated toward an inability to experience the universe as it actually is. We end up tearing apart the "garden planet" in our effort to redesign it.

If we were to accept the Earth on the terms and under the exquisite conditions in which it continues to evolve, the role of the farmer would be raised to a most honorable and sacred human profession. Relieved of the illusions that they are manufacturing food, or that they are worthy of success to the degree that they are also economists, cosmeticists, and managers, farmers might understand themselves as acting in something akin to a prophetic and priestly role. We need to see farmers as entering the sanctuary of the soil and engaging the mysterious forces of creation in order to bless and nourish the inner and outer life of the community they serve.

Villages, towns, and cities surrounded by farms practicing sacred agriculture would begin to regain the elemental prosperity of pure air, water, and diversity, and the possibility for health and vitality. The attention farmers would pay to the rhythms of the celestial world could reinspire the artists and poets. The music and texture of "place" would be grounded in the great seasonal cycles by which the human has been fashioned in our longing for communion with the Mystery at the heart of the world.

As our culture shrinks in its inner life and rages in violence between individuals and groups, and against the whole of nature, we might do well to reflect on the meaning of food. I do not believe that we are doomed to the inevitability of "engineering" food into a state of eternal shelf life, or that we must use our most deadly nuclear inventions to irradiate our food for its immortality. These compulsive tendencies can be changed.

We live in a universe with an inner spiritual reality. There is nothing that does not participate in this deep sacramental presence. The soils, the microbes, the animals are all holy, are all revelatory. Understanding the universe in this way has the capacity to transform our obsession with control and power.

It is my hope that the concept of sacred agriculture will find expression and authenticity on our land at Genesis Farm. By opening afresh the sacramental dimension of food, I hope to open the meaning of *Eucharist* and *Gospel,* so that we learn again to treat creation "knowingly, lovingly, skillfully, reverently" . . . as a sacrament. Let contemplatives return to the land.

✦ 22 ✦

A Spring Ritual

by LARRY PARKS DALOZ

Over the past several years, Sharon Parks, Cheryl and Jim Keen, and I have been studying the lives of people who have made long-term commitments to work on behalf of the common good. It turns out that many of these folks describe a significant moment or scene from their childhood that has stayed with them and served as a kind of inner beacon. Thus, a woman who spent her life working with Native Americans remembers being helped up from a fall in the mud by a kindly Native American man; a civil rights worker recalls being lifted up by the women in his church and declared successor to his father, the pastor; a philosopher of the environment recollects wandering for hours by himself in the woods. Knowing that such images at the heart's core can powerfully shape a life's dream, we have tried to offer our children a concrete vision with which to hold our shared love of the Earth.

One green May morning several years ago, my wife Sharon and I walked out with our two children into the woods above our house high on a northern Vermont hillside. We made our way some distance up through the mixed maple, spruce, and birch forest to a small clearing, seething with spring mud and fresh growth. Walking gingerly over the sphagnum and clusters of sundew, we reached a clear, sweet spring rolling up lazily from a cleft in the Earth just about large enough for a person to wriggle through were it not for the icy water flooding from its dark center. In silence, we knelt beside it for a few moments, and then, one by one, we lay down on our stomachs and drank. Faces barely above the water, we could look deep into the opening from which the water welled. Tiny grains of sand, now magnified into a miraculous watery other-world, teetered impossibly, balanced between the downward pull of gravity and the upward surge of the water, sculpting wondrous pillars, crests, tunnels. When we had drunk our fill, we arose one by one and walked slowly back through the sweet and silent woods.

We return to that source now every springtime. It has become a ritual for us. It seems important to know that there still remains such a place on the planet, and to keep it in our hearts—a place of clear and nourishing connection with the deep spirit of the Earth. This past May, as we knelt in the silence watching the water welling up limpid as we had remembered it from the year before, and the year before that, and the year before that, Todd turned to his older sister and said softly, "We'll always keep it this way, Kate, won't we?"

We can never be sure that Todd and Kate will be able to keep their pact, but we do know that the image of that clear, perfect water leading down and in has a permanent place in their souls. And we hold the faith that it will serve them well as a small beacon glistening in the forest as they make their way in the coming years out through the world and back home.

✦ 23 ✦

Responding to the Crisis

by FRITZ HULL

From where I sit each morning, in my favorite chair with my favorite cup of coffee, I observe a magnificent world. Living on the shores of Puget Sound in the old family summer home, I witness a splendid epiphany of nature. Often I watch eagles soar out over the water directed by the distant glint of a fish. Through the window I see otter, seal, porpoise, sea lion, and on occasion the Orca whales. Off in the distance to the east, my eye follows a vast stretch of mountains including a few of the highest peaks in the region: Mt. Baker, Mt. Rainier, and Glacier Peak. Below them lie the lesser peaks and hills with forests of fir, hemlock, and cedar. Just fifty feet beyond where I sit is the beach and the cold waters of the Sound, where I played and swam as a child, and where any time day or night I can, on simple whim, toss in my kayak and be off on an adventure. For most of my life this scene has impressed itself on my spirit and informed my sense of the world. I think how fortunate it is that I grew up here with a first-hand experience of the natural world. This world and all this beauty is still here, right outside my window.

From this same chair, however, I watch the encroachment of another world. For straight before me to the east lies a small city, once a lumber town, and now the home to aircraft construction and possibly a new home port for the navy. The hills behind that city, the foothills of the Cascades, are scarred by giant clear-cuts that become especially evident when it snows. On some days a brownish haze lies over the city nearly concealing the mountains. The waters of the Sound that touch that city and the shores of this island no longer remain clean, receiving the discharges of municipalities, the runoffs of fields, the spills and waste of ships, and refuse people carelessly drop into the water. Where as a boy I looked and saw mostly trees and beaches, I today see buildings, docks, smokestacks, and the sprawl of one of the fastest developing regions of the nation. All this is called "growth." The scene I knew as a child has become crowded with all the evidence of a civilization in powerful conflict with the natural environment. This, of course, is a scene repeated throughout much of the world.

For the past few years the conflict of these two worlds has been the focus of my personal meditation. I have come to realize that what I am watching every day is the story line of the modern age, the relentless overtaking and alteration of the natural world through human domination, manipulation, and consumption. For all the genius and good intent of this human advance, I now understand that I am witnessing from the comfort of my own living room a drama of destruction . . . the degradation of the beauty and integrity of the planet. At times I have felt a sort of depression watching and thinking about all this. How does one accept the enormity of this crisis and what it forbodes for the future? We have not intended all this damage. Can I see only the beauty and not the destruction, and thus split the two apart? Denial would be a handy and understandable option, but can be indulged no longer. The harm being inflicted upon the environment steadily worsens. I know, because while I am watching for the whales to pass by, I am at the same time observing the seiners haul in their diminishing numbers of fish, the tugs rafting logs to the mill, and the smoke of the city rising to the hills.

It is very possible that in a few years what most of us have considered normal may appear as really quite mad. Many of the things we think and do now will no longer be considered in anyone's best interests, and certainly not in the best interests of the Earth. Many of our assumptions will be under siege. We will simply be forced to make changes. Since responsible environmental information forecasts that what we now consider an environmental crisis may well become an environmental catastrophe, why do we wait to change course?

For what seems like a rather long time, I have reflected on the collision of the two worlds as witnessed from my window. Now I have watched enough. I am ready for a fresh round of action and remarkably, I am finding many others who are feeling the same. We are experiencing a readiness to draw on our inventive powers and courage and to bring a new urgency to our work. Like most of my friends, I haven't exactly been sitting around. We have been doing what we have known how to do. But there is a difference about this new time where challenge, hopefulness, and even enthusiasm have been joined. We feel definitely on an edge where there is new territory for us to enter and work to be done.

I am also ready to move because my questions have yielded some answers. It is my experience that living deeply into our questions draws us to a place in ourselves where we access a source of truth, compassion, and guidance. In that deep place wisdom reveals itself and we are offered a knowledge of how to proceed. It has become my experience, and therefore my conviction, that what we need to know in guiding ourselves and the affairs of Earth will be made known to us as we faithfully seek the necessary wisdom. In addition, I believe that we will find within ourselves the desire and the resolve to create what is now needed for our lives and what which will serve the lives of those who follow.

With a new determination to act and to make a contribution that somehow counts, I am definitely learning what next steps I am personally to take. In my prayer, meditation, journal writing, and in hours of reflective thinking I have been asking for wisdom. I have arrived at a point of believing that there are four basic things for me to do, and these form the foundation for my response to the environmental crisis. For me they express a broad and ecompassing spiritual content and tone. I believe that these are four proactive steps any of us can take. They are:

1. *Radical openness.* To stand before the real facts of our time demands a courage we may not have known was required of us. To assess our true situation, to see with eyes open the damage we have inflicted on the life systems of the planet, is hard work. It is not

easy either mentally or emotionally to stretch our hearts and minds around the extent of the havoc being done to the Earth and to watch it proceeding at an accelerating rate. Yet, any truly effective efforts to change our course and to create new and sustainable ways of thinking and living, demand a new honesty . . . an inner openness that allows truth to enter.

To keep from feeling overwhelmed and helpless many people decide they can bear only so much pain. To protect themselves from being discouraged by bad news they may limit the amount of disturbing data. Hence, they may also listen to those who will refute it, or at least give it a positive spin. However, as potentially risky to our future as the damaged environment itself, is our propensity to deny our true condition. Denial born of fear could become our greatest danger.

Determining our true condition is not limited to a description of things gone wrong. Just as true is the enormous capacity we have, both as individuals and as a culture, to make things right and to draw forth from ourselves the power of love to create new vision. To ignore this capacity, to trivialize it as being overly positive, is only another form of denial. In a culture where cynicism is rampant it is often easier to let in the bad news as to affirm much good news. It may require more courage to summon our hope and determination to persevere with positive action than to do little and worry more. Anxiety comes easily and positive action requires discipline. Necessary now is a thoroughly honest and steadfast affirmation of our personal capacity to be powerful instruments of change in our world.

A radical openness includes the belief, or the awareness of the possibility, that the power in the universe that has brought the world into being and has carried history to this point upholds us still. This is to affirm the words of the old hymn: "'Tis grace that brought us safe thus far, and grace will lead us home." Those of us who believe in the transcendent power of love and truth, which moves through all creation, are counting on the fact that this power is active always on our behalf. It also works in us and through us and we proceed into the future in a disposition of fundamental trust. Remaining vulnerable to truth allows our inner guidance system to give us self-correcting signals assisting in our next steps. The ability to be sensitive to this inner guidance is the work of prayer. It is the discipline of attunement from which our actions find power and direction.

Radical openness is the invocation of full-bodied living, of first-hand experience. It is being unafraid to immerse ourselves in the full drama of being alive at this cusp in history, and to become participants in this great transitional moment as we move into the twenty-first century. It is not wanting to miss what's going on. For me, the spiritual dimension of life has always been equated with total self-giving of energy and vigorous involvement. As a Christian I have known this element of wholeheartedness to be at the center of historic faith. I have heard it said that there are three kinds of people in the world: those who make things happen, those who watch things happen, and those who ask, "What happened?" Radical openness, in its essence, is wholeheartedness. It is lowering the threshold of fear, entering fully into life and trusting that we are competent to make things happen in a manner commensurate to the demand of the future.

2. *Changing Course.* Now is the time to have the nerve to do things differently. Environmental literature is filled with warnings that our patterns of consumption cannot continue if the natural world is to retain its integrity. A discerning but radical openness to this information challenges us with the knowledge that we cannot proceed as usual. To avert ecological catastrophe and enormous human dislocation and misery, a course change is required.

Our new course acknowledges that in many respects we were not on a good course in the first place. Only slowly have some of us begun to question our patterns of consumption. In preparation for the Earth Summit in 1992, the United States actually tried to remove the topic of consumption from the agenda of issues to be considered. Many Americans still seem largely unwilling to discuss or even imagine the longer term consequences and the true cost of the way we live and its affect on the Earth.

Once becoming open to our true situation, and understanding that our present course is one of acute danger, changing course becomes an issue of seeing what truly matters. Many in this culture are determined to maintain the present course just as long as possible and will attempt to rescue themselves only at the last possible moment. Others profess to see little danger. Some actually seem to want catastrophe, believing in it, as some fundamentalists do, as an article of religious faith. Still others see danger approaching but appear to be unable to take clear and decisive action, like a deer frozen in the headlights. Sometimes, when attempting to take action, environmental issues have been very narrowly conceived. Probably thousands of organizations have satisfied themselves that they have made significant changes when finally, often after considerable discussion, they converted from Styrofoam cups to an alternative. While it feels important to affirm that every action counts, in terms of the larger scale environmental disasters under way in the world, such efforts may be of little actual significance. The intention may be good, the direction important, but the scale renders too much discussion of things like a few Styrofoam cups an exercise in self-delusion, thinking we are acting responsibly when, in fact, we have failed to grasp the enormity of our predicament. We have not seen what really matters. Our tendency to obsess on small issues needs to give way to an enlightened grasp of complex global issues in a way that they remain present and powerfully active in our imaginations.

One of the great deterrents in this culture to managing a swift course correction is that people wait for someone else to go first. Yet, it is very difficult to go first, especially for people of relative affluence. For who thinks that they want less? Scaling down can be a forbidding prospect. But many people would do it if they saw others around them doing it, or *someone* doing it. A friend or some credible person in the community, has to create a new pattern and then call others into similar action. For many it feels like an issue of fairness, wishing for some kind of group action where many others are simultaneously stepping back from the brink.

Today it is critical that more people go first, taking the initiative to ease back and to discover that it is not necessarily a fearful thing to live on less, and very possibly to discover that it is actually a welcome and liberating experience. Acting in ways that are mindful of the greater whole, of the Earth and all its species, is not an unpleasant experience as some must suppose. It may not even be that difficult. Once the momentum builds in the new direction of what we must do, then some things may be surprisingly easy. Many people actually want to change course, their personal course and the course of the culture. There is a new readiness to make changes. It is now likely that individuals who will step out and initiate change will precipitate a long-anticipated awakening of consciousness and corresponding action.

3. *Intimacy.* As the environmental crisis has become alarmingly evident, and we have begun to search for causes, it has become clear that whatever might be the immediate catalysts of the crisis, the real causes run deep. We have begun to see that the underlying reasons for the crisis touch the very core of how men and women in the late twentieth century actually think about the natural world. Deeply ingrained patterns of thinking and behaving are hard for us to comprehend with objectivity. To imagine ourselves much differently is difficult. Yet, the enormity and growing danger of the ecological crisis demands deep level reworking of basic patterns of thinking and acting. For our task cannot be simply to ameliorate symptoms, but to solve systemic problems.

The word *intimacy* suggests both our problem and its solution. In Western culture over the past three hundred years, or since the rise of the industrial revolution, we have physically, psychically, and spiritually withdrawn from nature. We have walled ourselves away from a primary relationship with the natural world that as a species we have always experienced up close. Some cultural historians believe that this process started even much earlier with the rise of farming and settlements that became cities. This separation from nature seems to have occurred wherever humankind exercised various forms of manipulative control and domination over nature. Eventually we cocooned ourselves in human-built environments and away from the forces and elements of land, sea, and sky. We lost the intimacy of a firsthand relationship with the living Earth. In whatever way we trace the roots of this process of distancing and domination, the price of our alienation has been heavy. The extent of the damage to the Earth, as well as to our own selves, lies beyond comprehension. Perhaps there has been a certain inevitability about the path humans have taken, and some argue it has been in some respects necessary for our own evolution. Yet, for all our brilliance we are now living with the unfathomable consequences of our mistakes.

The intimacy we now seek is not a reversion to an older way of thinking and living. But moving successfully into the next century requires a reawakening of an instinctual affinity for being *with* the natural order, and the fulfilling of a psychic longing for being *with* the forces and elements of the created world. Nothing but a revived intimacy with nature will satisfy this deep hunger of the human spirit. As this hunger is met, we will experience within ourselves the beginning of the healing and transformation that will release the imagination and the desire to change our course and live differently upon the Earth. I believe that this relationship is charged with the energy of creation itself. This connection gives us access to the power to set us free from our present myopic disorientation, and to experience an immersion in the greater community of all life.

This is a difficult edge for those in various faith traditions who wonder if immersion in nature as a spiritual act is approaching a pantheism that would substitute nature for a relationship with God the Creator. Not at all. It is simply to affirm that the love and truth of the Creator God moves in and through all creation, and that the divine intention for all life and history is mediated to us in every moment and in every aspect of creation. Increasingly theologians and biblical scholars are becoming aware that the experience of intimacy with the natural world has long been a vital part of their traditions and needs to be reappropriated as a dimension of their disciplines.

The past few decades have witnessed an extraordinary emphasis on the individual and on issues of personal growth. A vast assortment of workshops and new therapies have focused intensively on personal health and empowerment. While much of this has been healing, some of this activity has also resulted in an inordinate self-focusing, and at times driven individuals deeper into separation from others and from nature. With such emphasis on the individual there has been little demanded in terms of exercising a loving responsibility toward others and the world.

It is now being recognized that participating as partners in a wider set of relationships is a matter of both individual and ecological health. Being lively members of the Earth community into which we have been born is both our calling and our source of strength. We are learning the ways that empowerment comes through relationship, and we now need to seek this by moving from the excessive self-focusing of the past years to a more extensive and inclusive experience of the world. Joanna Macy describes this as a movement from the ego-self to the eco-self, that is, to the ecological self.[1] Feeling our way along the intricate web of life, and learning our place in the order of things, is a critical act of self-empowerment. Extending our compassion to the whole of the Earth community will bring in return the inner strength that we sought all along. Intimacy with creation is a condition of personal empowerment.

To call ourselves to a new intimacy with nature requires a new definition of "nature." Nature cannot be limited only to what is "out there" and appears to us as pristine scenes and interesting animals. Nature is the wild storm, the exploding star, the violent volcano, and the ever-devouring food chain. Nature is the very life coursing within us, and it is also our death. Nature is what we see dancing under the microscope and the mystery that drives our computers. To behold these manifold worlds, and to allow in ourselves the essential experience of the awe, beauty, and sufficiency of the universe, is to enter a relationship with "nature."

What about an intimacy with things? Native Americans have long understood and taught a basic attitude of respect for all things, both living and nonliving. It is critical that things take on more importance, not less. They can even be extended a quality of sacredness. Respectfully taking care of things can mean we will have fewer of them. We won't have more things around than we can take care of and handle with respect. In our throwaway culture, an ethic of respect for all things would be subversive and threatening to our consumer economy. Respect for all things may be the most potent idea any of us has in meeting the environmental emergency.

A new intimacy is filled with knowledge as well as feelings of affinity and belonging. I'm quite sure that I have run many a workshop where people were sent into nature to reflect or meditate on their personal lives. This did not necessarily bring anyone closer to the world of nature, but often used nature to reinforce the self-focusing. Can we bring ourselves now to meditate *with* nature, as part of nature, learning of nature? This task includes building a knowledge base under our experience. On the island where I live there are forest trails I know quite well where I have walked for years, sometimes preoccupied with personal questions. Only when I walked these same trails with foresters and Native Americans did I realize how much I didn't know about where I was. I am learning now to enter the forest with lots of new questions and I carry on a great conversation, but not just with myself and about myself. Rather, the conversation is with what I see and encounter along the path. I am engaging my eco-self.

If disconnection from nature is at the heart of the mounting environmental crisis, then we have no time to lose in thinking, feeling, and weaving ourselves into a new pattern of intimacy. Our efforts may at times appear awkward to ourselves and others. We have no alternative but to experiment, and to challenge ourselves with the task of discovering the very thing that our inmost spirit seems to long for . . . the experience of feeling close, and that we belong.

4. *A Creative Response*. What can I do? This is such a liberating and empowering question when asked with the true inner willingness to act. An equally liberating and empowering answer can be: make it up, think up something. Make a creative response.

The mid-1990s could well be a period of intense and unusual creativity, a period somewhat like the early 1970s. The 1960s is remembered as a period of severe challenge to prevailing thought forms and institutions, exposing issues and demanding change. This was followed by a decade when many people worked to create positive alternatives for the concerns they felt so profoundly and were willing to roll up their sleeves and act in a spirit of high resolve and invention. Creativity truly flowered in the early 1970s and lots of people I knew began to create alternative energy systems, political strategies, publications, communities, gardening methods, construction ideas, schools, therapies, businesses, and health practices.

Leaving my work in campus ministry in a local church congregation, I moved to a rural area with my wife and son and a small group of friends to create an alternative form of religious and spiritual education. In 1972 we created the Chinook Learning Center on Whidbey Island in Washington State. We spent nineteen years with a community of learners offering to the public countless courses, workshops, conferences, and special events dealing with issues of personal spiritual empowerment and creative service in the world. The experience was enormously rewarding. Looking back on the effort to create an educational model, I feel our best work was the dedicated *intent* to create a model. Over many years we held to our commitment and we were successful in remaining creative people. We stayed with our task and our belief that God's Spirit was on the loose and that there was "new wine" flowing in our historical moment. It was our calling, we felt, to make "new wineskins" adequate for the surging creative potential of the time. I remain grateful and inspired by our efforts, for we gave ourselves wholeheartedly to what we loved and believed in. We saw what we were doing as our form of service to God and the planet.

Living during the Cold War, with the threat of nuclear holocaust, left many citizens with the feeling that there wasn't much anyone could do to change things. The issue seemed too big and distant and beyond our ability to affect the historical circumstances that held us in the grip of such a fearful possibility. By contrast, with the environmental crisis, we can see how each of us is a direct contributor to the problem often through patterns of overconsumption and waste. Fortunately, it is also easier to make the link between the problem and creating solutions where all can participate and anyone can initiate. All are welcome in crafting solutions, it's a game that any number can play. This sense of direct participation in both the problem and potential solutions is bound to arouse our desire to be creative. For some, a creative response might be to extend what we already do well, into some new form. This would involve taking the knowledge, professions, and skills that we already have and imagining a new way to utilize them in healing the Earth.

In these demanding times it takes a discipline of heart and mind to stay open not only to ominous environmental information, but open as well with a clear-eyed resolve to do something about it. Perhaps nothing is more critical than to make sure that while acknowledging feelings of helplessness, we decide to act on another set of feelings that includes confidence, trust, and the inner urge to make a creative contribution. This is a critical moment in which we need to encourage each other, and to pass the signal that this is our time to emerge with something to say and something to do. Everyone can make a creative response.

These four proactive steps grant to the human species a place of respect and high responsibility as we move from an anthropocentric to a biocentric vision of the world. We as humans, in spite of our record of stunning and incomprehensible abuse, are essential members of the Earth community. In whatever manner we may wish to define our uniqueness as humans, it is critical to affirm that we are the creators of new vision, and increasingly we bear responsibility for the future of the planet. This role should not be identified as hubris, though our propensity for this quality is well established. Rather, men and women have a distinctive and creative role among the Earth's species in helping guide the Earth community on its cultural and evolutionary path. As individuals we must acknowledge our complicity in destructive patterns of dominance and abuse, but debilitating shame will not serve us. We must pursue our high calling with both the necessary humility and the genius that lives within us as a species.

As essential as a high regard for the role and function of the human, is the attitude of respect and mutuality we extend to each other throughout the human family. We who live in the developed countries of the "North" are growing in an understanding that the environmental crisis frames and defines all other issues. As the future unfolds, the intensity and pervasiveness of this crisis will determine the shape and relative importance of everything else in our lives. The future will, indeed, witness us following Vice President Al Gore's dictum that the environment must become the organizing principle for everything we do.

Many people of the developing countries of the "South" find it difficult or impossible to embrace this view, or when they do it is with far greater anguish than people of the developed countries may yet feel. Their issues begin with the experience of crushing poverty. Until recently it has been common for the South to view the environmental crisis as being created by the North and concluding that the problem belongs basically to the industrialized and affluent countries. Their first concern is often survival and therefore their focus is development. During the Earth Summit in Rio de Janeiro in June of 1992 the entire world witnessed this debate. As I attended the United Nations Conference on Environment and Development and other conferences and events taking place during that historic gathering, it seemed to be clear to most everyone I met that it is unwise, unfair, and impossible to move ahead without these two issues of environment and development being inextricably linked. They are inseparable both ethically and programmatically. Therefore, those of us in the North who seek to be spiritually sensitive and environmentally active must also encompass even more in our compassion, grief, and creative imagination. For those people who have less and are demanding development, will be afflicted by enormous and disproportional worldwide environmental damage.

The Earth Summit itself was truly a remarkable event. Well over forty thousand citizens of the world and 118 heads of state came together representing 172 countries. It was one of this generation's great historical happenings. There was a palpable sense of something unprecedented and momentous underway. The Earth Summit now lives in the collective awareness of the world as an event where peoples from nearly every country came together in a unique forum. They sought a heightened awareness of the growing danger to the planet and a deepened commitment to live in economic sufficiency for all in a healthy environment. In the future we may gratefully observe that this event was a critical turning point for the health and ecological integrity of the planet.

It is essential that we learn from those who still live close to the Earth, or who maintain various forms of interactive relationships with the natural world. This can include farmers, hikers, poets, fishermen, astronauts, naturalists, biologists, landscapers, skiers, and gardeners. While the logging industry itself is under severe challenge, we will do well to understand that often loggers themselves have a substantial knowledge and respect for the forest. All those who know something about the natural world are needed voices. Those who view the Earth from centuries of tradition, as do the Native Americans, are especially needed at this time. The Earth-centered beliefs and practices of the original peoples of this continent are critical to the larger culture. Listening with respect and seeking to protect native people's rights and practices is a way of ensuring the health and future of both human and Earth.

Living on the shores of Puget Sound I have become accustomed to the dependable rhythm of the tide rising and falling. It is like many rhythms of the natural world; the return of the seasons, the phases of the moon, and trees growing, dying, and becoming seed logs for new trees. Such rhythms create a sense of trust that there is a "right" time for things. There are certain rhythms in the mood of our national life. Many parts of our cultural experience have spent their usefulness. Some ways of thinking and acting must begin afresh. A mood of helplessness and even depression is now giving way to a new spirit of hopefulness and a desire to take responsibility for our difficulties and to create solutions. We have arrived at a time of no less danger, but a time where increasingly our minds are being freed from the constraint of feeling too small for the challenge. We *are* strong and empowered individuals. Required of us now is the ability to empower ourselves as collectives, teams, and communities and learn the experience of synergy where the effect of our efforts together exceeds what can be accomplished separately. We simply have no time to lose in moving into this new spirit of hope and to act with boldness both individually and together.

As we move into a demanding future we must seek an even greater empowerment. Our ancestors sought the inspiration and guidance of the loving power that upholds the universe, that created the Earth and gave us all life. God has been known by many names, but has always and everywhere been sought for the resources that the human venture has required. People before us sought wisdom from the Earth itself when their future seemed uncertain or dangerous. For thousands of years men, women, and children gathered around the fire discussing their situations, wondering what to do next. Elders met around the fire and took counsel. They sought wisdom, created plans, and took action.

I have grown more confident that *we* will discover the needed wisdom and learn the ways to become resourceful and visionary members of the Earth community. As we learn a new love for this world, for nature in all its dimensions, we will meet our challenge and know what to do. For that which we love we will protect, defend, and heal. This is not a time to hold back. This new time requires imagination, love, and boldness . . . the pouring forth of our creativity into the life of the Earth, its peoples, and its future. Nothing less is required, and nothing less is in our best interest.

✦ *24* ✦

The Power of Our Grief

by JOANNA MACY

O ur planet is in trouble—and we know it. We know about the devastation of our forests and our trees. We know about the poisons that are leaching into our soils and seas and air. We know about the spasms of extinction that are wiping out our fellow species at a rate never before chronicled. We know about the exponential rate at which the forces of destruction, set lose by our kind, are eroding our very life-support systems. We know it in our bones. And we know this is a time of challenge we must face together if we are not to go under.

We know we must now learn new steps and strategies. How to live ecologically, how to live sanely and simply. How to organize effectively, how to start moving more and more toward a system that is sustainable, without which we can now see there is no life, no future. We know that by our intention bold new forms can break through, burst forth—new institutional forms, new ways of confidence, new ways of justice, new ways of economics, new ways of farming, new ways of being together, new ways of being on our Earth.

Where do we find the power for this, the power that can lead to the healing of the world? I think we find it in our pain, our pain for the world. We find it in the grief that comes over us as we see what is happening, the fear that takes us, the rage that swells up. Honor it. Do not think that this is a private craziness. Know that this is life itself crying through you. Let us be bold to acknowledge our grief—to own it—knowing that our grief and our rage and our fear for all beings at this time is our deepest health, our deepest sanity, the other face of love.

There is a gospel in our grief. It says we care. And that caring springs from our profound interconnectedness—an interconnectedness that weaves the web of life out of which we come, a web out of which we cannot fall.

The power that is there for the healing of our world doesn't come from any one of us. As we venture out the power is there. You see, we only need to let the amazing power of self-healing of our planet come through us. And where do we tap into this power? In our story, in the very journey that we have lived in our lifetime. In our lifetime as Gaia, the planet. This power comes as we drink from the deepest wells of the spirit and hear the song that has been sung through us since time began. The song that burst forth in the forming of the galaxies. The song that sucked biology out of the brimming rocks and that peopled our planet with the exuberance of life forms. This is what sings in us now. And we want it to be kindled, to hear it again stronger. Now that we, in our long planetary journey, have become graced with self-reflexive consciousness, we take glory in those roots and we can let the song sing through us.

✦ 25 ✦

The Power of the Individual

by JOHN GRAHAM

For most of my professional life I've been on the "other" side of the key issues from most of the people who are now my friends and collaborators. During the 1960s and 1970s I was a US Foreign Service Officer, specializing in political-military affairs. For fifteen years I was engaged in wars and revolutions and arms sales, either on the ground in tough situations in the Third World, or back at the other end of a teletype in Washington or New York. I know a lot about getting political results in an imperfect world.

At a certain point in my life—the classic midthirties crisis—I realized that I couldn't continue doing what I was doing, helping fuel endless cycles of mindless violence. That realization had been jabbing at me for years, but the adventure and glamour of my job always shoved it back to a far corner of my mind. It took the incredible violence of Vietnam to bring it so far forward I could no longer ignore it. During the height of the battle for Hue, in May 1972, with death and destruction all around me, I helped the South Vietnamese set up firing squads to shoot deserters and looters from the South Vietnamese army, who were terrorizing the city from the inside just as the North Vietnamese were attacking it from without. In helping one set of Vietnamese shoot another set of Vietnamese so they could get on with shooting a *third* set of Vietnamese—in a war I had long regarded as stupid and unwinnable—I finally recognized the irresponsibility of treating life as one big amoral adventure. People were living and dying because of my actions—now, right in front of my eyes. I had to take responsibility for what I was doing with my life. I had to probe what I believed in, to a far deeper level than I ever had before.

Gradually, my ideals and thoughts sharpened, but the process took a long time. Five years after Vietnam, in my last assignment in the foreign service, I was a deputy to Ambassador Andrew Young at the US Mission to the United Nations. In that assignment, I helped forge important initiatives to fight apartheid in South Africa, to secure the freedom of Rhodesia, and to help promote the Carter administration's agenda for human rights worldwide. I was at last on a track that served life instead of destroying it.

But that still wasn't enough. There were important changes I needed to make in my life, but I was too scared to take the leap. I was brave enough to leave the security of my government job, in 1980, but not brave enough to launch the real life's work that awaited. I knew that new work was there and beckoning, but the risk of accepting a change so great was too much for me. I needed a major shove.

I got that shove on October 10, 1980. Convincing myself that I needed some "downtime" after leaving the foreign service, I had signed on as a lecturer on a cruise ship, the SS *Prinsendam*, sailing from Vancouver to Tokyo. On the night of October 9, the *Prinsendam* caught fire in the Gulf of Alaska, and began to sink. The ship was abandoned; all the passengers and crew were put aboard lifeboats. At dawn on October 10, helicopters flying 150 miles from shore bases began to lift people out of the boats, one by one, at the end of long cables.

The helicopters worked fast, because a typhoon was coming on. By 4:30 that afternoon, only eight men, including myself, were left in Lifeboat Number Two, in what were now thirty-foot seas. The helicopters could no longer fly in the howling gale. With no protection from the storm, and no warm clothes or rain gear, we would die of exposure. Our only hope was that a Coast Guard cutter might find us, like a needle in a haystack, in the fury of this violent storm.

I tried to make my peace with the death that now seemed imminent. But I just got angry at God. Here I was, having finally made all these wrenching changes in my life to do good work, to do

God's work, and I was being wiped out before I even really started! It all seemed dumb. Then that anger gave way to a realization, prompted by a very clear voice that seemed to boom out of the storm. That voice said that I was still playing life as if it were a game; that I was eager to talk about my ideals, but still not serious about putting them into action. If I was going to continue to misuse my talents, the voice continued, I might as well end my life out here in this storm. But if I was willing to get *serious* about pursuing my true life's work . . . well, the choice was mine.

I got serious. And in that instant a Coast Guard cutter lunged out of the storm, coming straight for us. So help me, that's the truth.

I made good my promise. I went back to New York and began lecturing and leading workshops on political change, mostly for peace groups. I made every mistake in the book, but I was committed and it was a start. In 1982 I met Ann Medlock, who had just started the Giraffe Project, an organization that finds and honors people who are "sticking their necks out for the common good"— whom it calls, naturally, "Giraffes." The project gets the stories of these Giraffes told over local and national media, inspiring other people to get into action too, on issues of concern to *them*.

The Giraffe Project soon combined both Ann's work and mine. Since 1983 I have been its executive director. Some people call us a "press agency for heroes." We also design and implement *Standing Tall*, a program teaching courage and service to kids. Our Giraffe-a-Town Campaigns help towns and small cities tackle the toughest problems they face. And since 1989 we've backed "Giraffes Russia," based in Moscow.

I've learned a lot from the over seven hundred men and women we've honored on how to make a positive difference in the world, no matter what the issue. I'd like to share some of those lessons, plus some from my own life. I use my own life as a source because those fifteen years I spent dealing with the political and bureaucratic systems that support violence in the world gave me a very good understanding of the nature of power and conflict, and of how people behave in situations involving both. Over the last twelve years, I've spent a lot of time figuring out how to use that knowledge and experience to help other people in their efforts to make things better, for other people, and for the Earth. Here are my conclusions:

1. The core of successful social, environmental, and political action is being able and willing to take risks. Take a look at this morning's paper. Think of all the problems in your community or in the world that aren't being handled well—recession, homelessness, pollution, drugs, failing schools, decaying cities, a political system that many people no longer trust—all of us are familiar with the challenges of our times.

But why do these problems seem so intractable? We are an inventive people. We also are a caring people—most of us would like to see things get better, for our society as well as for ourselves.

What's lacking most is public-spirited courage. "Getting involved" in a public challenge is often risky—so most citizens stay on the sidelines, more adept at pointing fingers of blame than at taking responsibility, more likely to whine their complaints than to get to work on the problems. Too many people still believe they have no responsibility, that the problems are insoluble, or that others will do it for them. It's that reluctance to risk, to get involved, that's the problem—not a lack of brains or good intentions. We need more people with ideas and ideals who are sticking their necks out to put those ideas and ideals into action.

It's not just adults who need to take up this challenge. Too many of our children are now growing up with little commitment to service and responsible citizenship. The media bombard young people for hours every day with images that all too often are inane, selfish, and blaming. The very passivity of the hours that children spend watching television trains them to live their lives as spectators, not participants. Teachers and child psychologists tell us that the traditional idealism of youth is losing out to materialism and apathy, with dismal repercussions for the nation's future.

2. Using role models is the most powerful way to get people to take risks. Remember how much easier it was to jump off the diving board for the first time when someone just like us went first? Now the risks we are asked to take are more important, but powerful role models do exist. The Giraffe Project has been finding courageous, responsible, caring leaders and telling their stories through mass media since 1982. These Giraffes are people like Ed Benson, who roared out of a comfortable retirement to fight a toxic waste incinerator that was making people in his community sick; Janet Marchese, who has placed hundreds of newborn infants with Down syndrome in loving families by ignoring bureaucracies that said she couldn't do it; and Abdullah Turner and Nero Graham, who led their neighbors in driving drug dealers off their block.

Individuals like Ed, Janet, Abdullah, and Nero, by their example, help others see that they, too, can dare to act—can clean up the environment, renew their communities, take on problems of poverty and drugs and poor schools, and create a more peaceful world. Their message is that our lives count, that our ideas and values count, and that our voices and actions can make a difference.

3. The mission is not your project or my project—it's creating a "critical mass." We all know that all the problems we worry about are connected at their core. We need to deepen our realization of these links, and to realize that their solutions are linked too. The mission is to get enough people committed to courageous, compassionate service so that we create an unstoppable momentum for change, a chain reaction that will make sticking our necks out the norm, whether the issue is environmental, social, or political, whether the project is yours or mine. The popular phrase for this phenomenon, borrowed from physics, is "critical mass."

Successful changes in the way a whole society behaves rarely proceed on a steady, upward path. Rather, results are hard to see at first, as an idea slowly spreads, gathering proponents. Then, when that critical mass of people commits to the new way of thinking, the prevailing attitude in the society changes, often with astonishing speed, and a self-sustaining momentum develops behind the movement. The end of colonialism, the abolition of slavery, the success of the women's movement, and changed attitudes toward smoking, are all examples in which the building of a critical mass of people has created major change.

But the challenge now is not in solving any single issue. The challenge is in replacing carping passivity and feelings of power-lessness with active responsibility and courage—and to do it on the full range of issues that are shaping our lives.

4. Understand and use the power of caring to create change. As I know so well from my own life, we can take risks in many directions, some frivolous or harmful. Adding the element of caring provides the normative rudder for risk taking. It guides us toward risks that serve other people, and serve the larger whole—the community, the nation, the planet.

The bad news is that caring can in some people be so deeply buried that it is invisible and unusable. Indeed, much of our current (especially male) culture trains us to ignore or suppress caring in favor of more "realistic" behavior—like violence. The good news is that caring is always present in any of us, suppressed or not. In the tough world of the foreign service, I never met a human being in whom the caring instinct wasn't present, no matter how deeply buried. Serbian gunners killing women and children in Bosnia, for example, care for their own families; but, blinded by their fears and ignorance, they do not extend their care to a wider reality.

I use the word *instinct* deliberately. In the foreign service, when I saw caring survive in conditions that seemed totally uncaring, I realized that caring had to be more than just an emotion. With the right encouragement, it kept popping up, like the reflex action when the doctor strikes our knee with the rubber hammer. I eventually came to the conclusion that this caring reflex, this instinct, must represent some innate sense of our own connectedness to each other—that we humans understand at a very deep level that, in caring for others, we are caring for ourselves. Carrying it one last step, I came to see that this understanding is yet another proof of the connectedness of all life, of all there is.

This discussion is very relevant to successful action in the world. We all face seemingly uncaring "opponents" from time to time. If we believe that caring is in fact absent in our "opponent," then a win/lose situation is inevitable. But if we know that caring is there, even though buried by fear, we open up the possibility of much better outcomes.

Caring can be an enormous source of political power, *especially* in situations when caring is tough: such as caring for the developers who are destroying the Amazon rain forest or paving over a park in our hometown; such as caring for racist neighbors and infuriating bureaucrats and impossible coworkers. It's vital to care for opponents like these—not because it will get us into heaven, but because it will help us get the results we want here on Earth.

It sometimes mystifies me that more people haven't figured out the incredible political power of caring. I remember the scene in the movie *Gandhi* when, at the point Gandhi knows he has won, he is summoned to see the governor-general. Gandhi is in his loincloth, the governor-general in his dress uniform. Gandhi walks up to him and says, "As one man to another, sir, I want to apologize for all the trouble I have caused you." This is no ploy. Gandhi means every word. The governor-general, as he has been for the entire campaign of nonviolence, is dumbfounded and offguard, unable to play the usual power game.

Gandhi's actions worked because he never doubted that, using the power of his own caring for *both* Indians and British, he could find and strike that reflexive chord of caring in both. His compassion led people on both sides to tap into the source of what connected them on a much deeper plane than political aspirations in India. Tapping into that source led individuals on both sides to summon up their own compassion. That allowed both sides to establish just enough trust of each other to permit a lasting political settlement. The settlement wasn't perfect, but considering the disastrous clashes that ended colonialism in many other parts of the globe, Gandhi was a model of what humans at their best could do, and an inspiration to other leaders, such as Dr. Martin Luther King.

Gandhi and King, as master politicians, also clearly understood that the power of caring comes in part from its shock value. In basing a political strategy on caring, we are creating what is for many "opponents" a whole new game; it's a game they don't control, and they are offguard. But if we give way to hate and anger, if we move with cynicism, we are back to playing the old game, and our "opponents" probably know how to play that old game better than we do.

So let's not be afraid to change the rules of the game. If we're battling mill owners who say they would "like to eat spotted owls for breakfast," we need to find a way to talk to them, sympathetically and effectively, about their concerns for lost jobs and lost livelihoods, including their own. We must mean every word, and follow through. We need to establish enough trust so that both we and the owners can begin to see economic and environmental options that simply couldn't be seen in a climate of fear and suspicion.

A final reason for caring for our "opponents" is simply to maintain our own mental health. Sometimes it's necessary to fight hard to reach a goal; that's fine. But it's not fine if the fight is fueled by hate. It's not fine if our passion for doing the right thing becomes nothing more than bitterness toward the situation or our "opponent." The Department of Energy officials who lied for twenty years about the nuclear wastes at Hanford, Washington, may be low on our list of friends, but they're human beings too. They are human beings who made mistakes, terrible, arrogant mistakes, under pressure. If we forget their humanity, we undermine our own peace of mind and our own power.

5. *Take the risks of being responsible.* I don't just mean being responsible for that important political effort we may be involved in. Large and public political efforts must grow from, and reflect, smaller and more personal ones. Everything is of a piece. It's all connected. For some people, the most responsible thing they need to do is to go home and fix their relationship with their spouse or children. For some, it may be an ethical problem in the office or organization that's festering. As we tackle these personal crises, it's important that we don't end our participation in, or responsibility for, the larger efforts we're involved in. We must do both at the same time. Healing ourselves and our relationships, and healing our communities and our planet, are essentially the same process. We will succeed or fail in both together.

6. *Make sure that everything you do is personally meaningful to you, in terms of your own deepest values.* To be politically effective it's important that we deal satisfactorily with our own search for inner meaning. Isn't it true that when our work or activities have real meaning for us, there's a sense of excitement, fun, and passion that's not otherwise there? When it is, we are more inspiring to others and are better leaders.

On the other hand, there are times when we are caught doing work that isn't meaningful. There's little passion or joy. We're not very inspiring. We don't do our best job. Sometimes it's hard to get the job done at all. There's a natural yearning in all of us to do things that are meaningful, and there's a great emptiness when we don't. Some people try to fill that emptiness with possessions or drugs or power. Others might take on so many social action commitments that they lose track of why they are doing what they are doing. Either way, sooner or later they end up going through the motions.

If living and acting with meaning are that important, it's important to ask where the meaning in our lives comes from. Let me answer with an often told story about a management consultant who is sent to interview workers building a great cathedral many years ago. The consultant spots three people working on the cathedral. Two of them are stonecutters and the third is an elderly woman whose job is to sweep up the pieces of broken stone. The consultant goes up to the first stonecutter and asks him what he's doing and why. The worker looks exasperated and says, "Can't you see, I'm a stonecutter. It's a job. It puts meat on my table." When the consultant asks the second stonecutter the same question, he answers, "I'm making a gargoyle and it's going to go on the church someplace." When the consultant asks his question of the woman, however, she looks to where the huge towers will someday rise long after she is dead. Then she turns and replies, "I'm building a cathedral, for the glory of God."

It makes all the difference in the world how we see what we do. People working with real meaning in their lives, like that woman, don't look for that meaning in their job or activity, nor in their position or their possessions. In fact, they don't look for it outside themselves at all. Rather, they look for meaning *inside* themselves; then they pull it out and *apply* it to their job, or activity or marriage or study. The meaning they find and then pull out of themselves comes from a commitment to ideals bigger than themselves and their own needs. The ideals that consistently seem to provide meaning over the long term are ideals of service—to others, to communities, and to the planet.

Living our lives without sufficient meaning is intolerable. So it's important to ask ourselves continually some tough but simple questions: Am I satisfied with the level of meaning in my life right now? In my work or activity? What ideals am I willing to commit to, to provide that meaning? Am I doing all I can to work for those ideals?

When we do find that there *is* real meaning in what we're doing, then we mustn't be shy about it. We must never describe it as "just something I do." We must let it become a mission. Commitment at that level provides the passion and power and excitement we see in people who lead meaningful lives.

7. Learn how to form and communicate a powerful vision. A vision is a clear, concrete picture of the results or conditions we say we want. A vision acts as a source of guidance and inspiration. If a vision is powerful enough, it will attract resources to the effort, sometimes as if by magic.

From my experience, there are four key attributes of a powerful vision. We must make sure that our vision for a better world,

- is concrete and crystal clear. We must see it, taste it, smell it, touch it. If our vision is for ending homelessness in our town, then we must see, not just a new shelter (if one is needed) but the smile of relief on a homeless mother's face;

- is big enough. If our vision is banning a toxic waste dump in our town, then we must make sure that our vision of success includes all the other communities we will inspire and instruct with our effort, and the contribution our local effort, combined with many others, will make to the healing of the Earth itself;

- includes changed attitudes and not just changed policies. After the Valdez oil spill, it was important that the vision of environmentalists include not only cleaning up Prince William Sound, but also new laws and policies on the transport of oil. It was and is vital that that vision include changing the attitudes that *caused* the crisis. I don't just mean introducing a new sense of responsibility to governments and oil companies. I mean also changing our *own* attitudes as a people toward energy conservation. I mean very basic, everyday attitude changes that lead to more recycling, more car pooling, and turning off the lights when we leave the room;

• includes a picture of ourselves as role models for the changed attitudes we want to see in others. People need role models to think and act in a new way. And if not us . . .?

8. *The real risk is not dealing with fear of failure, but with fear of success.* Sticking our necks out for our ideals can be scary. But the time comes when we just can't talk about it anymore. We need to commit ourselves. As the old Chinese proverb says: "It's very dangerous to try to leap a chasm in two bounds."

Failure is possible, and it's not much comfort to be told that there are "important lessons" in the failure. It still hurts. But we're all grown-ups. We pick ourselves up, figure out how to improve our act, and begin again. When I see people pull back from putting their ideas or ideals into action, however, I often sense that it's not because they're afraid of failure—but because they're afraid of success. Here's what I mean:

When we tackle a challenge with the personal qualities I've been discussing—caring, responsibility, and meaning—and when we commit to a powerful vision and then take action, we experience a power and clarity that changes our lives. We watch ourselves in action and we realize, deep down, that if we're going to continue, we're going to have to give up the old and comfortable pictures we hold of ourselves, with all those limitations we thought we had: "I'm not bright enough, nice enough, strong enough, well-spoken enough, old enough; I don't have the time to do that; someone else will know better what to do."

We begin to see that these excuses are no longer true, if they ever were. So there's no way around the choice now in front of us. If we're going to continue to act at this level, we must confront head-on our own capabilities, and our responsibility to be leaders, role models, and agents for change. We must accept that we are that powerful and that our lives can be that meaningful. As we do, we sense that we are tapping into a power that transcends us as individuals. In my opinion, this is an invitation to an active and credible participation in our own divinity.

This can be the most frightening idea of all and there are no easy answers for dealing with that fear. It is a call to truly live our potential on this Earth. The challenge is as much spiritual as psychological. All we can do is reach into that very deepest part of ourselves and say, "Yes, I'll take it on."

None of us must back away from letting our lives be as important as they need to be. So let's get to work! Let's care, especially for our opponents, and use the power of that caring to get the results we want. Let's take responsibility for everything we do, or don't do. Let's put personal meaning in everything we do, based on commitment to our own ideals. Let's create and use a powerful vision of the results we want. Let's be ready to say yes to our own power and success.

Does this strategy *always* work? No, of course not. Everyone definitely takes a few lumps. But, from all my experience, I've never seen or used a more powerful means to get results. I *do* guarantee that following these principles will improve the odds for success, no matter what effort we're involved in.

Remember, too, that the world is desperate for role models, people living their lives with meaning and passion, because they are effectively linking their ideas and ideals to positive action. As *we* act in this way, serving life and serving the Earth, many others will be watching. The challenges may be large, but the prospects and possibilities are enormous.

✦ *26* ✦

New Story/Old Story: Citizenship in Earth

by PAUL GORMAN

I'm told I'm made of stardust but it doesn't feel that way. Getting up in the morning, I don't find myself looking in the mirror, thinking, "Primordial Flaring Forth." That subtitle of Thomas Berry and Brian Swimme's book, *The Universe Story*, inviting us into the Ecozoic Era, more nearly describes some petty outburst of household irritability than the outset of "the universe venture." "There he goes again," sighs my wife after some episode in the kitchen, "Ol' Primordial Flaring Forth." Hey, I'm just another Cenozoic guy, and you know where I live? New York City. We specialize here, you might have heard, in being ontologically undifferentiated cosmos in conscious self-celebration. Come on down.

We have our moments, actually. Last night, I stopped twice to talk to homeless men panhandling. One was a Vietnam vet. He'd look for a job, he told me, but just had no money to buy clothes for an interview. I gave him my "spare change" and said he deserved better. He nodded blamelessly, and actually replied, "Keep hope alive." The other was an older guy, too old for this. I told him I'd been tapped out by a younger brother down the block. As if he knew him, he said, "That's fine, can't feed everybody." There was straighter eye contact with them than most days at the office. I didn't need a New Universe Story to get next to those two guys.

What kept me next to them keeps me next to the Hudson River, or to the faint smell of sea at the arrival of a low front, or, without much effort now, to the rats that scamper in and out of my building. Bare attention, open heart, commitment to communion with whatever is right in front of me. I'm up for entering the Ecozoic Era—but not in some romanticized pastorale, not without the company of those two homeless men. I need to enter in citizenship and solidarity. And these interactions have been no less ruptured than those more "elemental" flows within the biosphere.

All we have been stripping from the natural world we are also stealing from our own public lives. How fares the web of life? Well, how fares the family? Where *is* the family? Where are my neighbors? *Who* are my neighbors? Didn't we all used to have more friends? The natural fabric is being rent, and is it a surprise that we're left feeling lonely?

Citizenship entails consent. But by whose decision, through what collective deliberation are entire species of the planet being killed off . . . how many per week now? Life is disappearing; shouldn't we expect to feel radically disenfranchised?

Citizenship flourishes as a natural expression from within a genuine commonweal. But everything that we unquestionably should share merely by virtue of being here—water, air, soil, fish, fowl, flowers—are these in any way held in common and in trust? How can we expect to share equitably the hard won wealth of human labor when we cannot even conserve what we were all given for free? The commons are robbed; what else in the wake but loneliness, clinging, and greed.

Do we think our assault on the natural world would leave our civic life untouched?

But if these two worlds are intimately connected, it must follow that the practice of citizenship has something to contribute to healing in Earth. So how to be a citizen in a biocidal age? Here's a question this book might send us all out asking. For me, for the moment, it seems at the very least to require a posture of inquiry into what must be made new again, and recollection of what must not be forgotten, and generally being okay with not being quite sure.

If we are to work in nature's name, we might start out with nature's cues. Embrace diversity. Observe law. Respect process. Care for what is bequeathed. Seek symbiosis. Ally abrasion. Stay in scale. Rest. (And rest a little more.) The challenge, in other words, would be to restore citizenship, not only as action on behalf of ecology, but somehow as the practice of ecology itself. That would mean not only organizing, voting, demonstrating, writing letters—not simply action "out there" about stuff "over yonder." It would invite citizenship from "in here," from within the natural order, drawing where possible on its appropriate images and life-enhancing instructions: cocreate, sow deep, cultivate, fertilize, connect, replenish, vitalize, cleanse, heal, draw forth, give birth, bury, recycle. I take these as civic virtues that can be consciously accorded value as we define and enact nitty-gritty political work.

But citizenship is still a human enterprise, and there is unfinished business in how we view the place of the human itself. Addressing this question—seeking to get the species back in scale—has been the preeminent contribution of such "New Story" thinking as appears in these pages. But I have been having my own little mind-dance with the politics of much "Earth spirituality." Where's *human* suffering in this story? Aghast at anthropocentrism, have many turned to efforts on behalf of nature to avoid facing our failure to heed and heal one another? Is there some new self-hatred at work here? Back to the garden only to rediscover the shame? What we've learned about human citizenship at its best we can't dispose of in our disgust at human behavior at its worst.

That effort isn't any easier when we try to find appropriate political strategies. So much environmental activism has been dry or uninformed by the deepest spiritual impulses of our best new thinking. I'm all for the Environmental Defense Fund weaning McDonald's from Styrofoam, say, but it doesn't quite ease the yearning. And the dualism of more confrontational action seems to violate precepts of communion that ought to be at the heart of planetary healing. But then I find myself flying over New York City on the night of riot in Los Angeles, and the power-plant smokestacks below suddenly turn into great hypodermics shooting smack into the skin of the sky. The culprits and victims of poverty and pollution seem the same. And I'm thinking petrochemical executives are criminal and just plain have to be brought down. "By any means necessary." Yet seconds later, quieter, I find myself asking if we really have no choice but to work with these guys, help them see what they're doing, give them "incentives"—only to realize, to my horror, that these turn out to be incentives to barter "pollution rights." Sigh. I pause, watch a few breaths, resolve to hold on to some essential militancy, dig in on my own work, make peace with ambiguities, and know that there'll be room and time to see more clearly what's called for and what works.

And again in new citizenship's name, I turn to past struggles. I understand what's behind Tom Berry's suggestion that "democracy is a conspiracy against the natural world." I know he's puckish, and enjoys needling us, and I take the point. But there is a noble history of democratic thought and struggle that has moved for centuries toward an increasingly inclusive vision of citizenship. Through it, slavery was abolished, the universal franchise secured, the right to organize unions guaranteed, human rights assured, equal protection of the law, freedom of speech, assembly, the right to freely worship, the right of women (still up for grabs) to make decisions affecting their bodies. No small undertakings. Someone said, "Let's put an end to the divine right of kings." Imagine how it first felt to take on that struggle. Less daunting at the time than seeking to preserve the biosphere now?

People sacrificed and bled and died. And they were people like us—who had dreams and doubts, unsure of what they had to offer and what it would take, had sick friends to care for and got sick themselves, never saw the full fruits of their labor, simply went forth and engaged history, took one step and then another until it became a path.

We are in their debt and in their lineage and that's the Old Story and it's still true. The New Story, of course, is that suddenly there is much more than human well-being for which to struggle now. But then there is so much more with which to feel solidarity. All life.

The effort to newly discover appropriate citizenship, then, can be a vehicle for discovering proper human place. It will be a journey, a climb. But there will be moments, almost certainly unexpected, when we will be given images of hope and promise.

My friend, Drew Christiansen, recounts a visit with a fellow Jesuit to our first national monument, the Pinnacles, where on a winter camping trip, clambering through caves and canyons, awed at the natural history, approaching the top of his last climb, he suddenly came upon what he called the most wonderful sight of the day: a group of handicapped people climbing the mountain, in wheelchairs, on crutches, or held by friends or volunteers, mostly women. There it all is, I thought, when I first heard the story: the wounds and the willingness, the struggle and the celebration, we humans grappling with and grappling within the rest of God's creation.

"That night," he reported, "as I sat under the desert sky, wondering at the plenitude of the heavens and all I had seen that day, Immanuel Kant's dictum came to mind about the two things that inspire awe, 'the starry sky above and the moral law within.'"

· 27 ·

A New Conversation
by FRITZ HULL, *Editor*

oncurrent with the creation of this book, I was privileged to gather regularly with a group of men for conversations about our lives in light of the environmental crisis and to seek wisdom together for the way ahead. The group is part of the Men and Nature Program of the Institute for Earth and Spirit, co-directed by two contributors to this volume, Kurt Hoelting and David Gunderson, who are authoring a book based on the insights harvested from these gatherings. Professions in the group ranged from carpenter to fisherman, lawyer to architect, YMCA executive to therapist. Participants were: Kurt Hoelting, David Gunderson, Doug Kelly, Dan Kowalski, Ross Chapin, Rick Jackson, Fritz Hull, Jim Shelver, Peter Evans, Dave Anderson, and Rick Ingrasci. While exploring personal issues, our group over and over focused on an intensifying concern about the destruction of nature, much of it by men, and for the future of our children. Our final discussion on a weekend in January 1993 seems a fitting conclusion to this book.

Kurt: You made the comment last night, David, while we were walking on the beach, that everywhere we look in our culture we see our own reflection. Since we all seem to seek situations of wonder and awe, why do we choose to live our lives in situations and circumstances that are so removed from the sources of wonder. What's going on? Why is that?
David: But are we ever removed from the sources of wonder? I

don't think so. Wonder isn't external to us. It's a quality of attention we bring to our circumstances.

Ross: So the question is, Can you experience wonder on the thirty-first floor of an office building chugging away on a keyboard?

David: Or doing dishes. Like Thich Nhat Hanh says, if you don't get it doing dishes, you're not going to get it.

Kurt: Even when I'm out commercial fishing I'm involved in an activity that is mediated by so many layers of technology that there is rarely a time when I'm there, wherever it is I am, without engines rumbling, without electronics giving me most of the information I need to know. It's rare just to *be* there.

Fritz: It sounds like the stories the astronauts tell, that it's not until something malfunctions, and they have to wait, sometimes outside the capsule. Something has to stop, and suddenly, they are awestruck by their view of the Earth. And boom! That's when it happens.

Kurt: So, even in a space capsule, with the Earth before you, you are still just seeing your own reflection, because you're interacting with the task at hand, with the agenda you've been given, the job description. You're still seeing only your own reflection.

Dan: Kurt, let me jump in here. I think there's a real tension in the question, namely, what are we as human beings? Well, part of what we are as human beings is this cerebral, problem-solving, social animal, that does these things as ants might do, and that's part of us. And in doing this, like the astronauts, we are preoccupied, and we might not then be able to be at one with the rest of what is around us. But the question you began with was, Why aren't we living closer to what gives us awe? I've always thought that I'm awestruck when I'm in the wilderness. That's something that's easy, and I can go and jump in a kayak and be there. For me, that's the easy way. But the hard task is to get there, to the experience of awe, on a more regular basis while fulfilling our social and professional obligations, or in whatever role we find ourselves.

Ross: I recently read *Reflections from the North Country* by Sigurd Olson. He writes about meeting people who had given themselves to the wilderness, who had been out there for a long time and had lost themselves. When they are out there too long, they lose touch. Then they are not in touch with this something that is *us*, with this deep humanity. Yes, it is important to go out into nature, but it is equally important to come back, and to be in the flux and flow of humanity. If people are just going out, something is lost.

Dan: Yeah. In Alaska it's called getting "bushy." When you've been out too long, you get bushy.

Doug: I think it's kind of wondrous to think how we got into space in the first place. Just the power of the image, of being able to see the Earth as whole. How about all the people who just literally thought about the fact that it could be done, and made it happen—the exertion of human will that caused that experience to happen!

Kurt: Yeah, and that is a wondrous thing. But my grappling is around the question of wildness. What impact do wild places, wild natural forces, have on our ethical thinking? Gary Snyder recently said that if being in a wild place, in and of itself, brought forth ethical thinking, then our great deep ecologists would have been the fur trappers of the Rocky Mountain Fur Company. Which is true, in a certain sense. But I'm not completely satisfied.

We're no longer in the situation we were in for thousands of years, when there wasn't a separation between the "wild" and the "human." This notion of "wilderness" as a place that is apart from human activity and culture is simply false. People lived in the world, and the world was wild, and the human community was included in that wildness. Now we have a situation in which we are living as if going to "wild places" is a nice thing to do when we have time, to get back in touch with something that is aesthetically pleasing. But otherwise, nature is not really an ethical backdrop. It rarely enters into what we define as important in making our great decisions.

So now, we come up against this rather staggering realization, that our religious beliefs are not survivable. Our belief systems are out of touch with the way the ecosystems actually work, and effectively we are in the process of defining ourselves out of the system that brought us into being. So in my mind, it's not just a question of where do we go for wonder, or how does the natural world nourish our sense of being in touch with a satisfying life.

It's a matter of having our very propensity to be active and creative beings destroying the whole world, because of this lack of remembering what the ultimate "nature" is in which our human nature exists. How do we work with this, when there isn't anything remotely resembling a consensus that this is the situation we're in? People live their lives in an electronic bubble that now includes "virtual reality," in which it becomes possible to convince ourselves that "nature" is a kind of two-dimensional thing out there that we look at, but that doesn't really have any bearing on the way we live our lives.

David: But I want at least to consider the possibility that it has always been that way, that when biblical people, three-thousand-years ago, talked about "hardness of heart," this is what they were saying: "You look at things and you can't see. Don't you see, you're passing by reality. Why aren't you engaged?" That's the two-dimensional backdrop. Maybe that two-dimensional quality is a stage of human consciousness that spiritual traditions from all different angles are saying we have to get beyond. You've got to wake up to your "original mind." You've got to be born again. You've got to connect. We've been struggling with this for as long as we've been talking about ourselves as human. So in some ways we're not dealing with a new problem.

Ross: We're talking about a new context in which we've reached the edge of the frontier. We've reached the end of the planet. Before, the planet was always endless, boundless. It's the same human story we've been going through. The only difference is that the context has changed. We've come to the other side.

David: Now we have to deal with our story.

Dan: I think we're getting at the nut. We are in a context now that is unique to our human evolution in that we realize that we have filled up the planet, and that continuing in our ways is, in fact, jeopardizing the health of all life. The work now is to come to terms with the ancient task of developing clarity and presence as human beings.

David: Things were spacious enough for a while that we could get away with a kind of sloppiness. But not now.

Kurt: So, on a personal scale, nothing has changed. We're still these human animals who are driven to be the way we are, forming families, working to provide, looking for meaning in our individual lives, looking for some security, enjoying nature to the extent that it fits with all those things. And in fact, we can't ignore all those basic things about ourselves. If we do, we're like the person Ross mentioned who loses himself or herself. That's not going to work.

On the other hand, there is something that is much more than just intellectual or aesthetic about the question, Where do we turn for ultimate verification of what we're about? How does that relate to this world of nature around us in which we live, that we have in recent times defined as apart from ourselves and there for us to use? How do we address that issue without denying or hiding from the technologies that we have and the sensibilities about the universe that science has taught us? It's a new terrain that we're in. And it truly is an uncharted terrain, that requires us to put those two together. How do we do it?

Dan: With rigorousness. I really believe that. I believe that each one of us as individuals has to be conscious, and try, and get up early, and try our best to do our part, and continue the process of divining what our part ought to be—to engage exactly what we're doing right now, trying to get at it, and form plans that might work. We need to tackle difficult cultural problems that we're up against, whether it's having to work real hard to make a lot of money to pay for this and that, it's all the work that needs to be done, and we need to do it with rigorousness. And I think this is very, very important. We're trying to get at it here. And if there's clarity that emerges then, by God, publish it some place!

Kurt: It's all a question of sustainable culture, of human nature in the context of wild nature, and how nature must become the ethical bedrock from which we need to be working.

*David:*When you talk about ethical bedrock you're really asking, "What order is there in the universe?" And how do we participate in it? How does that order speak to our apparent freedom, and where do we find models for making our choices and exercising our creativity? How do we realign ourselves with the ways that awaken in us a sense of wonder about being human, about being a natural creature? A splendid natural creature! Gifted. If only we could see that in each other, educate our children so that that's what is being addressed, so that we have some interpretive framework that we believe is true.

Doug: I think the whole question of ethics rests on some established parameters about what is acceptable, what's to be promoted, what kind of conduct, what kind of activities. As we go about the activities that are necessary to the human condition, where do we turn to find the moral basis for making those choices? Our ethics are laid on top of morality in a very intricate way in our culture.

David: It's like Ivan Karamazov said, "Without God, anything is possible." If the ultimate foundation of values disappears, then you're just deceiving yourself. It doesn't really matter. You shake hands or you run someone through with a knife. It's all the same.

Doug: It's in nature that we must find morality. It is in nature that we must find the underpinning that becomes the central tenet in an ethical order. I think it's what Al Gore said. I think that we *do* know. It is more widely known than we might have imagined, even if we don't act on it. For me, there is a sense now that we have an inkling of the ethics of the new order. And it is the environment. It is the Earth. This is the essence of what must form the foundation for the new order. And that's what all these questions are born out of, whether it's "right livelihood," or being out in nature.

David: Could you put some concrete examples to that? You as a human being, how do you learn to act ethically in the world, from nature?

Doug: Well, let me take what is an obvious example and that's the idea of being in space. I think the first inklings of what we're now finally beginning to act on came when we first saw a picture of the Earth, when we could all see it. I mean, we've known for centuries that the Earth was round. But what happened when we got out and saw it was that we began, in a very profound way, to *own* it. I remember years ago doing a workshop at Chinook with futurist Ed Lindaman talking about how you face the future, and holding this notion of "bringing Earth home." It ties in with the question, Where are you most at home? Well, I'll tell you where you *should* be most at home. It should be when you know you're on the planet. When you *get* that you're on the planet. That's where "home" is. It's not in the forest. It's not here on the beach. It's not in the mountains. It's when you finally can let your mind embrace the fact that the planet is your home. When you understand the planet is your home, then when you see what goes on in Somalia or Bosnia, it's like, my God, you're ripping up my front yard! It's that passion you might feel about tending your garden. You know, that is my garden you're ripping up!

So I think that ever since we started seeing those pictures, seeing the beauty of the planet, I think it started permeating our beings in a way that, up to that point, when we were just spinning those globes on the desk, we never quite understood. They were all just kind of funny colors, and the ocean was sort of a bad blue, and it had lines on it. I don't know what the green over here has to do with the red over there. That was it. That was the best you could do.

So I think it started back then in an almost subliminal way. And now, it's like ethics are as straightforward and direct as recycling. It's a mundane example, but recycling is an ethical choice, a decision to conduct your life in a certain way with the awareness that the stuff you have comes back. Now, think back twenty years ago, think to your childhood. Did you ever recycle anything? Was it even a word you knew? Was it something you even thought about? The stuff went somewhere in a dump, it stank, and the sea gulls dealt with it. It didn't connect up with what went on in the kitchen, that's for damn sure. There wasn't that bridge. And now it's there. Everything you pick up, the minute you pick it up, you hold it up and wonder, "Where's that going to end up? Is that a recyclable container?" So I think that is a concrete example of what I'm talking about.

And now there's the notion of business "going green," the idea that in order to survive in the marketplace, this is the way it ought to be. Now you have to know your business can be reborn, you've got to connect it with something that's whole. It's like the Earth itself. We've had this notion that progress is connected to the frontier and conquering the wilderness. I mean, we're going West, young man! That's where the new horizons are. And you just keep going out there, and you keep cutting and clearing, and pretty soon. . . . We've got to change our notions of progress, and that's a very, very hard thing to do. When you think of what this country was born out of, and where we started, it's just like remaking the myth of the future. That's where it gets tough.

And I'll tell you, in my view, the slowest, the very, very lowest vibration is the legislature. I mean, finally, when law changes, things have slowed way down, when they finally take hold of it, and they write it down and say, "Okay, now you're all going to do it." Well, somebody had the idea years ago! So, when somebody like Al Gore gets into the White House, or Bill Clinton, it's the result of an idea that has been coming down. But we still haven't really shaped the myth that in some ways we're already starting to live. I really think that now there is an opportunity. But, you know, we're carrying a lot of baggage and we need new myths to live by. I mean, you've got to get excited about realizing that we aren't here just by accident. Wonder is when you realize that, not only is it great that I can experience this, but I *own* this! Then, the idea of saving it, and helping it be born again, and again, and again—that's such a powerful notion.

Rick: And maybe just powerful enough to help us transform the marketplace, and also transform our own attitudes to survive the marketplace that continues to try to get us to buy another pair of socks to raise the GNP. All that you've been saying reminds me that it's not just ethics "out there," but also the ethics "in here," in terms of the choices and sacrifices we need to make for ourselves and our kids, that must be made with rigor.

I've been inspired in our conversations by the degree to which I've seen other men pursue their own courageous development, as writers, actors, educators, as livers of life, day-to-day, trying to find the places within our work and lives to take relatively more courageous actions or stands, or to live with the tensions.

Dave: For me, it's real interesting to see what other men are thinking about. Sometimes I wonder if I'm the only one who has these thoughts or concerns. When you find out you're not the only one, you feel a little less crazy, especially in this culture, where you can feel like an alien. It's comforting to have fellow so-journers.

Dan: I think of this group as a foundation, one of those places up in the Alpine where you find smoothed-off granite. I know I could call any one of you and get a good conversation on a question I'm wrestling with. And that's terribly important to know that there is this granite that I can touch, or base something fundamental upon.

Kurt: It has been clear to me that my community is dispersed in space, and the people who provide it for me aren't all right around me, and that it takes work to maintain the connections. I really need that bedrock, and when I look at the number of people around me who don't seem to have it, I feel incredibly blessed. My own desire and intention is to do what I can, to be able to answer my children's question in the future, "What did you do, back then when there was still some time—what did you do?" I feel, as most people do, overwhelmed about what is to be done, and I need help. That's what this group has been for me. It has brought together my own hunger for spiritual community, my need for other men with whom to be about my work in this world, and my sense that I've got to do whatever little bit I can to make a difference, to claim a future that's sustainable.

Fritz: I have felt from our first gathering a profound gratitude for this group. We have traveled a great distance in our eight meetings.

Peter: Fritz, can you speak to the qualities that distinguish this group from others?

Fritz: I would say that we have readily been able to transcend our own agendas, and accomplish far more than relating our stories, sharing our grief, and revealing very personal aspects of ourselves. We have also thought together about the Earth and our place and responsibility in the order of things. We did not get bogged down with inordinate self-focusing typical of many groups. As men we came together in a spirit of brotherliness, sharing our concerns and vision, offering mutual support, and determining to work together on behalf of the welfare of the planet and the future of our children.

Ross: Each of us seems to have gotten hold of our lives and we're asking, "What can I do? How can I serve? How can I make this world a better place?"

Rick: In our conversation we've quoted Gary Snyder several times when he talks about "the pain of the work of wrecking the world." But I think what we're all after is the joy of the work of healing the world—healing, and being healed by the work we share. How much we need to be supported in this, lest it be only work. Kurt, I also want to thank you for your question, perhaps the simplest and most profound I've heard, which is: "What am I going to tell my children?" I think it's a touchstone question for this group.

Jim: I was thinking exactly the same thing. I've been working on an outline for the presentation I'll be making to the people riding the Puget Sound ferries. I'll be part of a program helping to educate and raise awareness about the fragile quality of the waters of the Sound. I've been wondering what I can tell people who want to know why I'm doing this, and you've given me a beautiful way to say it: Did I do my part? Did I stand up for my seven grandchildren? How could people challenge that?

Fritz: I'd like to tell you a story about my early days in campus ministry, when I went to Selma. I had no intention of going there, but I sat in a meeting where the question was posed, "Who is going to go?" and everyone but me had a reason not to go. The next day I was on a plane to Montgomery, and on to Selma. I remember the whole thing so vividly because suddenly I was radically out of context—a fish out of water. The marchers had already tried to make the march several times, but they'd been beaten up. Finally, there was a Federal Court injunction and the march was made legal. Martin Luther King, Jr. himself cast the march as a great Exodus—leaving bondage and entering the promised land. I stood out in front of the Little Brown Church, our headquarters, and all the great leaders of the civil rights movement were there. As we assembled to begin the march, King addressed us telling us to remember that, "You will tell your children and your grandchildren that you were here."

One day, years later, my son Timothy asked me about Selma,

and I remembered what Martin Luther King, Jr. had said, and I told my son that I was there, that I shared in that historic moment. Someday our children and their children are going to be asking us about this time we are in, about this historic moment. And we are not going to look at our children and have nothing to say.

Notes

Preface by Fritz Hull

1. Chief Dan George, "My Heart Soars," *Earth Prayers*, Elizabeth Roberts and Elias Amidon, eds. (HarperSanFrancisco, 1991), p. 42.

Chapter 1: The Power of the Well-Packed Question by Vivienne Hull

1. James Stephens, *Irish Fairy Tales* (New York: Macmillan, 1948), excerpted in *Parabola*, D. M. Dooling, ed., volume 9, number 4, November, 1984, pp. 80–82.

2. Maurice Strong, "Our Common Future," an interview conducted for the Rene Dubos Consortium for Sacred Ecology at the Cathedral of St. John the Divine, New York City, 1992.

3. Gar Alperovitz of the North American Center for Economic Alternatives, in an address to a conference on "The Economics of Our Democracy: Values, Visions, and Action," sponsored by the National Network of Grant Makers, Chicago, November, 1992.

4. Sally McFague, "A Square in the Quilt," *Spirit and Nature*, Steven C. Rockefeller and John C. Elder, eds. (Boston: Beacon Press, 1992), pp. 47–50.

5. Ibid., p. 50.

6. N. D. O'Donoghue, "St. Patrick's Breastplate," *An Introduction to Celtic Christianity*, James P. Mackey, ed. (Edinburgh: T&T Clark, 1989), p. 54.

7. Ibid., p. 50.

8. Ibid., pp. 47–48.

9. Ibid., p. 62.

10. Mary Aileen Schmiel, "The Finest Music in the World: Exploring Celtic Spiritual Legacies," *Western Spirituality: Historical Roots, Ecumenical Routes*, Matthew Fox, ed. (Notre Dame, IN: Fides/Claretian, 1979), p. 185.

11. Richard Woods, O. P., "Environment as Spiritual Horizon, the

Legacy of Celtic Monasticism," *Cry of the Environment*, Philip N. Joranson and Ken Butigan, eds. (Santa Fe: Bear and Co., 1984), pp. 77–78.

12. Christopher Bamford, *The Heritage of Celtic Christianity, Ecology, and Holiness* (West Stockbridge, MA: Lindisfarne Press, 1982), p. 11.

Chapter 4: The Joining of Human, Earth, and Spirit by Daniel Martin

1. Thomas Berry, lecture given at the "Spirit of the Earth" conference (Wainwright House: Rye, NY, March 1991).

2. Brian Friel, *Dancing at Lughnasa* (London: Faber & Faber, 1990), p. 35.

3. Richard Leviton, "Voices from the Dreamtime" (*Yoga Journal*, September/October 1992), pp. 66ff.

4. Robert Pogue Harrison, *Forests* (Chicago: University of Chicago Press, 1992), pp. 200–201.

5. Laurens Van der Post, *A Story Is like the Wind* (New York: Morrow, 1972), introduction.

6. Thich Nhat Hanh, *Peace Is Every Step* (New York: Barton, 1991), p. 26.

7. Wendell Berry, "The Pleasures of Eating" (*East/West*, December 1990), pp. 51ff.

8. Alice Walker, *The Color Purple* (New York: Washington Square Press, 1982), p. 178.

9. The Earth Charter is the distillation of a series of consultations held throughout the world, organized by the International Coordinating Committee on Religion and the Earth (ICCRE) to elicit contributions from the religions of the world toward the creation of a UN Earth Charter. It was offered during the preparatory process of the United Nations Conference on Environment and Development (UNCED, June 1992), also known as the Earth Summit, for the purpose of influencing the Earth Charter agenda. It now stands in its own right as an interfaith perspective on the crisis we face and the future we must create.

Chapter 5: The Soul and the World by David Whyte

1. Reprinted from the book *Fire in the Earth* with the kind permission of Many Rivers Press, Box 868, Langley, Washington 98260.

Chapter 9: Reimagining the Role of the Human in the Earth Community by Sharon Daloz Parks

1. See Sharon Parks, *The Critical Years: Young Adults and the Search for Meaning, Faith, and Commitment* (San Francisco: Harper Collins, 1986).

2. Ibid. See chapter 6, "Imagination: The Power of Adult Faith."

3. Frederick Beuchner, *Wishful Thinking: A Theological ABC* (New York: Harper & Row, 1973), p. 95.

4. Sharon D. Welch, *A Feminist Ethic of Risk* (Minneapolis: Fortress Press, 1990), pp. 23–47.

5. See James E. Loder, *The Transforming Moment: Understanding Convictional Experiences* (San Francisco: Harper & Row, 1981).

6. Al Gore, *Earth in the Balance: Ecology and the Human Spirit* (Boston: Houghton Mifflin, 1992), pp. 117–18.

7. Ibid., p. 194.

8. Gaston Bachelard, *The Poetics of Space* (Boston: Beacon Press), p. xviii.

9. Joanna Macy, "The Greening of the Self," *Dharma Gaia: A Harvest of Essays in Buddhism and Ecology*, A. Badiner, ed. (Berkeley: Parallax Press, 1990), p. 56.

10. See Sharon Daloz Parks, "Home and Pilgrimage: Companion Metaphors for Personal and Social Transformation," *Soundings* 72.2–3 (Summer/Fall 1989), pp. 297–315.

Chapter 11: *The View from the Grounds by Kurt Hoelting*

1. Gary Synder, *Axe Handles* (San Francisco: North Point Press, 1983), "Dillingham, Alaska, the Willow Tree Bar," p. 91.

2. Timothy Weiskel, quoted from presentation at the Earth and Spirit Conference in Seattle, Washington, October 1990.

3. Gary Snyder, *The Practice of the Wild* (San Francisco: North Point Press, 1990), p. 61.

4. Richard Nelson, *The Island Within* (San Francisco: North Point Press, 1989), p. 123.

5. Snyder, *Practice of the Wild*, p. 15.

Chapter 12: *The Path of Place by Sheila Kelly*

1. Gary Snyder, from *Upriver Downriver* no. 10, as quoted in *Home! A Bioregional Reader.* Edited by Van Andrus, Christopher Plant, Judith Plant, and Eleanor Wright (New Society Publishers: Philadelphia, PA, 1990), p. 34.

2. Wendell Berry, *Clearing* (New York: Harcourt Brace Jovanovich, 1977).

3. Terry Tempest Williams, *Refuge: An Unnatural History of Family and Place,* (New York: Pantheon Books, 1991).

4. Gary Snyder, *The Practice of the Wild* (San Francisco: North Point Press, 1990), p. 39.

5. Snyder, *Home! A Bioregional Reader*, p. 5.
6. Snyder, *Practice of the Wild*, p. 41.
7. Snyder, *Home! A Bioregional Reader*, p. 70.
8. Snyder, *Practice of the Wild*, p. 41.

Chapter 16: Awakening to the World of God's Creation by Michal Fox Smart

1. This trip was sponsored by Olin Sang Ruby Union Institute in Oconomowoc, Wisconsin.
2. Sh'ma = lit. *listen*. A central affirmation in each of the daily prayer services. "Hear O Israel, the Lord our God, the Lord is One."

Chapter 17: Planting Seeds of Joy by Stephanie Kaza

1. Robert Aitken, "Kanzeon" in *Not Mixing up Buddhism: Essays on Women and Buddhist Practice* (Fredonia, New York: White Pine Press, 1986), pp. 24–29.
2. For evidence of this growing conversation, see recent issues of a number of Buddhist publications, including *Tricycle, Turning Wheel, Inquiring Mind, Vajradhatu Sun, Mountain Record;* and also essays on Buddhism and Ecology in *Dharma Gaia*, Alan Hunt Badiner, ed. (Berkeley: Parallax Press, 1990).
3. For example, the *Earth and Spirit* conference in Seattle (1990), the *Spirit and Nature* conference in Middlebury, Vermont (1990), and the Third International Buddhist-Christian Dialogue in Boston, with "Ecology and Religion" as a key theme (1992).
4. Thich Nhat Hanh, *Being Peace* (Berkeley: Parallax Press, 1987), p. 91.
5. Venerable Santikaro, *"Ariyasacca:* Buddhist Problem-Solving" in *Engaged Buddhism: A Manual for Social Change* (International Network of Engaged Buddhists, draft 1992), Paula Green and Stephanie Kaza, eds., pp. 106–10.
6. Impacts on women workers have been documented by the Center for Women's Economic Alternatives, PO Box 1033, Ahoskie, NC 27910.
7. For excellent writing on soil and agriculture, see *Meeting the Expectations of the Land*, (San Francisco: North Point Press, 1984), Wes Jackson, Wendell Berry, and Bruce Colman, eds.
8. For resources on her work, see *Despair and Personal Power in the Nuclear Age* (Philadelphia: New Society Publishers, 1983); and *World as Lover, World as Self* (Berkeley: Parallax Press, 1991).
9. Beverly Wildung Harrison, "The Power of Anger in the Work of Love" in *Making the Connections*, Carol S. Robb, ed. (Boston: Beacon Press, 1985), pp. 1–21.

10. Thich Nhat Hanh. *Plum Village Chanting Book* (Berkeley: Parallax Press, 1990). This includes the most recent revision of his original Fourteen Precepts, based on discussions with students.

11. Thich Nhat Hanh, *Present Moment, Wonderful Moment* (Berkeley: Parallax Press, 1990), pp. 9, 32.

12. Maha Ghosananda, "Cambodian Prayer" in *The Path of Compassion*, Fred Eppsteiner, ed. (Berkeley: Parallax Press, 1985), pp. 24–25.

13. Dalai Lama, *A Policy of Kindness* (Ithaca, New York: Snow Lion Publications, 1990).

14. Sulak Sivaraksa, *Seeds of Peace* (Berkeley: Parallax Press, 1992), pp. 62–72. Sulak advocates small *b* Buddhism as a foundation for sustainable development in Asian countries dominated by inflexible Buddhist hierarchies.

15. Dalai Lama, "Five-Point Peace Plan for Tibet," proposed September 21, 1987, in *Essential Environmental Materials on Tibet* (Washington, DC: International Campaign for Tibet, 1990), p. 50.

16. Dalai Lama, "Ecology and the Human Heart" in *My Tibet*, Galen Rowell, ed. (Berkeley: University of California Press, 1990), pp. 79–80.

17. These conversations will appear as a collection of essays, *The Attentive Heart: Conversations with Trees* (New York: Ballantine Press, 1993). The work is inspired by Martin Buber's thought in *I and Thou* (New York: Scribner's Sons, 1970).

18. Quoted by Peter Steinhart in "Teaching and Preaching" in *Audubon*, 1985, p. 10.

19. Bill Devall, "Ecocentric Sangha" in *Dharma Gaia* (Berkeley: Parallax Press, 1990).

20. From his lovely collection of *gathas* (many of which are environmental), *The Dragon Never Sleeps* (Monterey, Kentucky: Larkspur Press, 1990), p. 39.

21. Quoted by Brother David Steindl-Rast in a talk at Green Gulch Zen Center, 1992.

Chapter 21: Food as Sacrament by Miriam Therese MacGillis

1. Vincent McNabb, O. P., *Old Principles and the New World Order* (New York: Sheed and Ward, 1942).

2. Thomas Berry, *The Dream of the Earth* (San Francissco: Sierra Club, 1988), P. 215.

Chapter 23: Responding to the Crisis by Fritz Hull

1. Joanna Macy, "The Greening of the Self," Dharma Gaia, Allan Hunt Badiner, ed. (Berkeley: Parallax Press, 1990), pp. 53-63.

Acknowledgements

his book owes its origin and inspiration to a conference created by the Chinook Learning Center entitled *Earth and Spirit,* which was held in Seattle in October 1990. Attended by more than one-thousand people, with a large national faculty of scholars, theologians, native elders, environmentalists, and artists, it turned out to be an unusually successful and powerful event. Under the capable direction of Peter Evans, conference chairperson, and a core team of exceptionally skilled and dedicated people, this conference earned the praise of Thomas Berry, who concluded: "You get a conference like this once in a lifetime." From this event has come much of the material and spirit of this book. As a principal organizer of the conference my first thanks, therefore, go once again to the Chinook Learning Center and all who worked on this significant event. By your efforts you have made a major contribution to this volume.

This book would simply not exist without the vision and editorial work of my wife, Vivienne. We have labored side by side on this project and derived enormous joy from seeing this book emerge. Vivienne's skill with words and passionate commitment to making the spiritual dimension accessible and real is felt throughout this book.

Since there are twenty-five contributors, there is no doubt that quite a few people, unknown to me, have had a hand in helping some authors with the writing, typing, and editing process along the way. One I do know and want especially to thank is Peggy Harrington, assistant to James Parks Morton, Dean of the Cathedral of St. John the Divine in New York City, who put in untold extra hours helping to prepare the Dean's manuscript. Also of great help was Whidbey Island friend Sally Thompson, who transcribed many of the conference presentations for authors to begin their work.

The award for most inspirational player goes to Tom Berry. During the Earth and Spirit Conference he was honored as an esteemed elder by Ken Cooper of the Lummi Nation and gifted with a long-used ceremonial drum. For many years, Tom has been a friend, mentor, and generous colleague. When we first met the crisis of the environment was not widely recognized as a significant issue. Tom knew that it was. He had already been out and about for years speaking with wisdom and great heart about what was happening to the Earth, and the terrible diminishment of the human spirit that the degradation of the natural world would bring. In the ensuing fifteen years, many have heard the wisdom of this man and have been profoundly affected not only by his insights, but by his relentless commitment, vitality, and abiding affection for life. He has shown the way to me, and to many, and for his remarkable spirit I am deeply grateful.

As the work on this book began, I was happily impressed with the willingness of all the contributors to author a chapter. Each was eager to participate in this project and entered into it in a high spirit of collaboration. The time and effort of each one, and the personal support given along the way, are much appreciated. All authors also offered their manuscripts freely as a gift to support the newly formed Institute for Earth and Spirit. I am immensely grateful for this and, with the staff of the Institute, look forward to more collaborative projects with this outstanding group of friends.

The new Institute for Earth and Spirit, like this book, also has origins in the Chinook conference. The Institute is dedicated to extending the ideas, values, and principles expressed in this book into areas of public life, particularly the worlds of business, theological education, and various other professions. For information on the Institute for Earth and Spirit you may write to P. O. Box 529, Clinton, Washington 98236. Everyone who has contributed to this book has thus had a hand in launching the new work of the Institute. My gratitude to all.

Contributors

ALAN ATKISSON is a Seattle-based consultant, writer, and musician with a passion for sustainability, innovation, and cultural change. From 1988 to 1992 he served as managing editor and (from 1989) executive editor of *In Context*, an award-winning quarterly magazine focused on the same trio of topics. He now works with companies, government agencies, nonprofit organizations, and religious groups seeking to embrace the environmental, economic, and ethical imperatives of the 1990s.

THOMAS BERRY is a historian of cultures, associate professor emeritus at Fordham University, and noted scholar. He is the founder of the Riverdale Center for Earth Studies in New York, which is devoted to the study of a viable mode of human presence upon the Earth. He is past president of the American Teilhard Association for the Human Future. He is the author of numerous articles and books, including *The Dream of the Earth*, and coauthor, with Brian Swimme, of *The Universe Story*.

KEN COOPER—CHADASSKADUM, Native American, Coast Salish people, has walked Mother Earth for a half century, studying Indian botany and spirituality, and weaving these two worlds together. He is a cultural resource specialist for the Lummi Nation in Washington State, and is a Lummi traditionalist. He is a leading voice on environmental and forest issues in the Northwest and on behalf of indigenous peoples in other parts of the world.

LARRY A. PARKS DALOZ is an associate professor of adult education at Lesley College in Cambridge, Massachusetts. He served as a Peace Corps Volunteer in Nepal, an educational planner in New Guinea, and helped to found the nontraditional Community College system in Vermont. With his wife, Sharon Daloz Parks, and two other colleagues, he is currently conducting a study of the lives of people who are able to sustain long-term commitments to the common good in the face of global complexity. He is the author of *Effective Teaching and Mentoring: Realizing the Transformational Power of Adult Learning Experiences.* He is a trustee of the Institute for Earth and Spirit.

MICHAL FOX SMART is a graduate of Princeton University's Religion Department. After graduation she received a Fulbright scholarship in Jewish thought at the Hebrew University and studied at Pardes Institute for Jewish Studies. She is the founder of Yitziah: Jewish wilderness expeditions and environmental programs. She has spent the last year pioneering the field of Jewish environmental education and also served as an advisor to the Consultation on the Environment and Jewish Life in the spring of 1992. She recently married James R. Smart who shares her passion for wilderness.

PAUL GORMAN serves as executive director of the National Religious Partnership for the Environment, headquartered at the Cathedral of St. John the Divine in New York City. He holds degrees in philosophy from Yale University and Oxford University, where he was a Kingsley Scholar. He has served on the staff of the Senate Foreign Relations Committee and as public policy consultant to numerous elected officials as well as to the governments of Bermuda and Venezuela. For twenty years he has hosted a regular public radio program and is a popular lecturer on issues linking the environment and religious life. He is the coauthor, with Ram Dass, of *How Can I Help?: Portraits and Reflections on Service.*

JOHN GRAHAM is executive director of the Giraffe Project, a national program inspiring people to "stick their necks out for the common good." Before the Giraffe Project he was a Foreign Service officer for fifteen years, serving in Libya and Vietnam, and at the

US Mission to the United Nations. He left the Foreign Service to found Politics that Heal, a series of lectures and workshops on creating political and social change. He continues to lecture and lead corporate seminars around the country. An avid mountaineer, he lives with his wife, Ann, founder of the Giraffe Project, on Whidbey Island, Washington.

DAVID GUNDERSON was born in Seattle in 1952 and has lived for much of his life in the Northwest. Following undergraduate studies in literature, he went to seminary and was ordained an Episcopal priest in New York in 1981. He is currently a pastoral psychotherapist in Tacoma, where he lives with his wife and son. He is also a co-director of the Men and Nature Project of the Institute for Earth and Spirit, and he follows with intense interest the conversation between Christians and Zen Buddhists.

BARRY HEREM is a Seattle, Washington, artist and writer specializing in the landscape and Native American and Canadian art heritage of the Pacific Northwest coast. He is also a poet, outdoorsman, photographer, and performance lecturer. His art work in bronze, cast paper, serigraphs, and steel sculpture is influenced significantly by the Native tradition of the Northwest coast. His journalism, book, and art reviews have been published in *Connoisseur, Architectural Digest,* and *Alaska* magazines, in addition to many Seattle publications. He is currently at work on his first book, a biography/review of the life and work of artist Duane Pasco, to be published in 1994.

KURT HOELTING is a commercial fisherman and building contractor who divides his time between Alaska and Whidbey Island, Washington. He has a master of divinity degree from Harvard Divinity School, and is a student of Zen Buddhism. The father of two children, he is currently co-director of the Men and Nature Project of the Institute for Earth and Spirit.

FRITZ HULL is the founder and director of the Institute for Earth and Spirit and former co-director and founder of the Chinook Learning Center on Whidbey Island, Washington. He is a graduate of Princeton Theological Seminary and holds a doctor of ministry degree from San Francisco Theological Seminary. He is an ordained Presbyterian minister. With his wife, Vivienne, he is currently directing a study and authoring a book on "The Power of Innovation and the Revisioning of Religious Education." He also teaches, speaks, and consults with churches and organizations across the country on spirituality and the environment. Born and raised in the Northwest, he makes his home on Whidbey Island.

VIVIENNE HULL is the associate director of the Institute for Earth and Spirit, and a former co-director and founder of the Chinook Learning Center. Born and raised in Northern Ireland, she has made Celtic Christianity an area of special scholarship. She lectures and leads programs in the United States and Britain as well as annual retreats on the Island of Iona in Scotland. She is a Lindisfarne Fellow. With her husband, Fritz, she is currently directing a study and authoring a book on "The Power of Innovation and the Revisioning of Religious Education."

STEPHANIE KAZA is a Zen student of Kobun Chino Roshi and Thich Nhat Hanh, and practices at Green Gulch Farm and Jikogi Zen Centers. She has studied deep ecology and systems theory with Joanna Macy. She serves on the board of the Buddhist Peace Fellowship and is currently assistant professor in the Environment Program at the University of Vermont where she teaches environmental ethics. She has been a naturalist and educator in the California landscape for over twenty years. She is the author of *The Attentive Heart: Conversations with Trees,* a collection of meditative essays recently published by Ballantine.

SHEILA KELLY has spent the last twenty years working on environmental issues in roles ranging from grass-roots activist to state government where she served as assistant director of Public Outreach for the Puget Sound Water Quality Authority. She was the Pacific Northwest coordinator for the US Citizens Network for UNCED. She is a graduate of Gonzaga University in Spokane and holds a master of public administration degree in natural resource policy from the University of Washington. Her life and work now, as consultant and writer, are based in Seattle.

MIRIAM THERESE MACGILLIS, O. P. is a member of the Dominican Sisters of Caldwell, New Jersey. She is the director of Genesis Farm which she co-founded in 1980 as a ministry of her Dominican congregation. The farm is a learning center that assists people in their search for more authentic ways to live in harmony with the natural world and each other. In addition to programs in the New Cosmology and Earth Literacy, it focuses on experimental, biodynamic agriculture. Miriam also travels extensively, lecturing and leading workshops on the spiritual and practical aspects of the new cosmology.

JOANNA MACY is adjunct professor at the California Institute of Integral Studies and the Starr King School of Ministry. She is a scholar of Buddhist philosophy, general systems theory, and deep ecology. Her books include *World as Lover, World as Self; Dharma and Development; Despair and Personal Power in the Nuclear Age;* and *Thinking Like a Mountain: Toward a Council of All Beings,* which she coauthored with John Seed.

DANIEL MARTIN is founder and director of the International Coordinating Committee on Religion and the Earth (ICCRE), which created the interfaith Earth Charter. He was born in Belfast, Northern Ireland, educated in Ireland, and worked as a priest in Kenya for ten years. Since coming to the United States in 1984 he has worked at the United Nations Environment Program, completed a Ph.D. under Thomas Berry, and directed an institute in global issues. Currently, he is an associate staff member of the Institute for Earth and Spirit, works with the Soundwaters Project, and writes and speaks widely on the spiritual dimension of the ecological crisis.

JOSEPH W. MEEKER is a nationally known human ecologist, with a Ph.D in comparative literature, and a master's and postdoctoral studies in wildlife ecology and ethology. Through his work as a professor, radio broadcaster, and author, he has furthered the understanding of the vital connections between science, philosophy, and art. He is the author of several books including *The Comedy of Survival* and *Minding the Earth*. An avid hiker and lover of wilderness, he makes his home on Vashon Island, Washington.

JAMES PARKS MORTON is dean of the Episcopal Cathedral of St. John the Divine in New York City, which he has served since 1972. Formerly an inner-city priest in Chicago and New Jersey, he has gained wide acclaim for his pioneering ministry in ecology and the arts, as well as his work in promoting understanding among the world's religions. He is the president of the Temple of Understanding, co-chair of the Joint Appeal by Religion and Science for the Environment, co-chair of the Global Forum of Spiritual and Parliamentary Leaders, and chair of the Lindisfarne Association. Popularly known as the "Green Dean," he and his wife Pamela are the parents of four daughters and five grandchildren.

SUSAN OSBORN, born in Minnesota, is an internationally known vocalist, songwriter, and educator based on Orcas Island, Washington. She has performed in many countries, most recently in Japan and Germany. Her current album, *Wabi*, won the 1992 Recordo Taisho award for best concept in contemporary music in Japan. She is a former lead vocalist with the Paul Winter Consort. For over a decade she has also led workshops in which people discover the magic of singing and the power of unlocking their own voices.

SHARON DALOZ PARKS is senior research fellow in leadership and ethics at Harvard Business School and at the Kennedy School of Government. She holds a doctor of theology degree from Harvard Divinity School and is the author of *The Critical Years: Young Adults and the Search for Meaning, Faith, and Commitment*. With her husband, Larry Parks Daloz, and two other colleagues, she is conducting a study of the lives of people who are able to sustain commitments to the common good in the face of global complexity. She was a founding member of the Chinook Learning Center and is a trustee of the Institute for Earth and Spirit.

WM. JAMES RILEY is a Cascadian priest, poet, and philosopher who lives with his family on Whidbey Island, Washington, where he delivers the rural mail, teaches philosophy at the local university, and conducts rites of passage for people in transition. He is a former Jesuit priest and professor of philosophy at Seattle University in Seattle.

DAVID SPANGLER is an internationally known author, lecturer, and educator. He is a former co-director of the Findhorn Foundation in Northern Scotland, founder of the Lorian Association, and is a Lindisfarne Fellow. He has also worked as a consultant and game designer for a number of game companies, including Lucasfilm Games, Inc. His books include *Revelation: The Birth of a New Age, Emergence: The Rebirth of the Sacred,* and *Reimagination of the World,* coauthored with William Irwin Thompson. He makes his home in Issaquah, Washington, with his wife and three children.

BRIAN SWIMME is a popular author, lecturer, and educator who is the director of the Center for the Story of the Universe at the California Institute of Integral Studies in San Francisco. A mathematical cosmologist educated at the University of Oregon, he is the author of *The Universe Is a Green Dragon* and the video series "Canticle to the Cosmos." His most recent book, *The Universe Story,* is coauthored with Thomas Berry.

DAVID WHYTE is a poet, writer, educator, and world traveler who leads tours to Nepal, the English Lakes, and the Galapagos Islands. Born and raised in Yorkshire, England, he now makes his home on Whidbey Island, Washington, with his wife and son. He is the author of three books of poetry, *Songs for Coming Home, Where Many Rivers Meet,* and *Fire in the Earth.* His most recent book, *The Heart Aroused: Poetry and the Preservation of the Soul in Corporate America,* will be published in January 1994, by Doubleday/Currency.